PURPOSE Killers

Exposing the Hindrances to Purpose

'PURPOSE' killers

Exposing the Hindrances to Purpose

Dr. Rhonda J. Ferguson

ISBN: 0-87148-472-2
Library of Congress Number: 2004103780

© Copyright 2004 by Rhonda J. Ferguson
All Rights Reserved
Printed by *Dereck Press*, Cleveland, TN

CONTENTS

Chapter	Title	Page
	ACKNOWLEDGEMENTS	2
	INTRODUCTION	6
1.	FINDING THE ROAD TO PURPOSE	16
2.	OBEDIENCE	30
3.	SEASONS OF PURPOSE	41
4.	PURPOSE AND PEOPLE PLEASING	49
5.	PASSION: THE FUEL FOR PURPOSE	62
6.	THE KILLERS OF PURPOSE	68
	DISTRACTIONS- Suffocation of Purpose	70
	PROCRASTINATION- The "Silent" Killer	76
	GIVING UP- Destruction Of Purpose	82
	THE BACK DOOR-	91
7.	PURPOSE AND YOUR LINEAGE	101
8.	THE POWER OF PURPOSE	112

ACKNOWLEDGEMENTS

To God be the glory for the things He has done! All praises to my Lord and Savior Jesus Christ for giving me the strength, determination and wisdom to do His will.

To my husband Anthony, Thank you so much for your assistance and encouragement. Thanks for the words of wisdom you have given me, thus enhancing God's purpose for my life. Despite the trials and tribulations that life brings, you are STILL the man of my dreams. Thank you for being a great husband, a wonderful father and my best friend. I love you.

To my children, James Marquis (#33 represent), Christian, Brendon, Anthony Jr., and Mikhaila. Thanks for allowing Mommy the time to write this book. You are all my princes and my little princess. Continue to seek God's purpose for your life. Mommy loves you all.

Special thanks to my godchildren, Starlanda McGill, Latoya Jackson, Tomika McDougald, Shawn Hoggs, Nate and Daniel Wilson, and all of Capital District Youth Mass Choir. You guys have done so much for me. I thank you so much for all your support, assistance and love.

To my parents and first teachers, Robert and Janie Franklin (my Poopa and Mommy). Words cannot express how I feel about you. I am the product of you both stepping into purpose. Thanks for the 6 a.m. prayers! Thanks for never giving up on me. Mommy, continue to believe God for your healing. Daddy, thank you for taking care of Mom. I love you both.

To my in-laws Clarence and Esther Ferguson and family, thank you both for accepting me into your family and treating me as your own. You have given me the greatest gift, your son. For this I am truly grateful. Thank you Papa for correcting my English!

To my Godmothers, Nan Motley and Joan Gray, thanks for nurturing and looking out for me.

To my siblings Robert (Ann) Franklin, Leonard Watkins, Donna (Bob) McLendon, Linda Watkins, Trina (Edsall) Walker, Robin (Timothy) Craig. Thank you for all that you have done for your "baby" sister. You all really mean a lot to me. I love you guys. To my brother-in-law John Campbell, I thank you for being the greatest husband to my sister, the late Andrea D. Campbell who I love and miss dearly. Thank you for loving and taking care of my sister. You will always be my brother-in-law.

To my sister/cousins Theresa Surgick, Rose Odom, and Denise Odom-Gabourel and my brother/cousin Benjamin Odom, Jr., thanks for your support and encouragement. Uncle Ben, I thank you too for supporting everything that I have done. I appreciate you so much.

To all of my nieces and nephews, you know that I love you. You all are so special to me. Continue to seek God's will for your lives.

To Claxton and Michelle Wilson, thanks for being there for us through the good and bad times. I love you guys and appreciate you for everything.

To the "Golden Girls" Kim Dyson and Yvonne (Peter) Rice, my childhood friends. Your friendship is amazing. Thank you for being a part of my life.

To Deborah Ann Smith, I will never forget how you looked out for my baby and me. Thank you so much.

To my pastors, Crosby and Rose Bonner for opening my eyes to the Kingdom! Much love! Even though we are many miles away, you will always be our pastors.

Thanks to all the pastors and churches that have allowed me to minister and serve your congregations over the years. You have certainly imparted God's Word into my life.

Thanks to Jerry Puckett for taking a chance on me. I really appreciate you for this.

Special thanks to Elaine Penn and Esther Bost for your prayers and constant encouragement. Special thanks also to Herbert Snowman, Carol Collier, Kristy Alicie, The Lakeforest Middle School family and all donors who contributed to this project.

I could go on and on acknowledging the numerous people who have impacted my life over the years. To those unnamed people, please know that I love and appreciate what you have done for me. I pray God's blessings upon your life.

This book is dedicated to the memory of my sister and brother, Andrea D. Campbell and Ronald L Franklin, Sr., grandfather Algae Jacobs, aunts Delila Odom and Virginia Hoffler, nephew Jason E. Mayo, my little cousin Patrice Gabourel and my mentor Rudolph V. Stinney.

INTRODUCTION

"IT IS TIME FOR YOU TO STEP INTO YOUR PURPOSE! GOD HAS CALLED YOU TO DO A MIGHTY WORK!" How many times have you heard this statement? How many times have you prayed about this and still nothing has changed?

For the last year or so, I have been preaching on the subject of **"PURPOSE"**. No matter what the theme or topic, I still end up on the subject of "Purpose". For some reason, I cannot get away from this subject. However, it does not stop there. Whenever I turn on the television to watch my favorite Christian broadcast, I would come across some man or woman of God instructing the viewers to "find their purpose."

After hearing my sermons on purpose, many people would come up to me and ask, "How do you get started?" In the last year I have seen people go to the altar after being convicted, begging and pleading with God to show them what He wanted them to do. After spending time at the altar, many of them would go back to their seats, seemingly unsure or confused. Had they heard from God? Some asked why had God not "spoken" to them as He had spoken to others. They wanted God's will for their lives so badly that they would go to the altar every chance they had. For many, this ritual would continue over and over leaving them feeling as though they've come up "empty handed" every time.

After witnessing the plight of these people, I found myself asking God many questions. What is so important about finding purpose? God, being who He is, will accomplish whatever He wants anyway. Is He not Sovereign? Therefore, why is it so important to know and find one's purpose? If purpose is so important then why does it appear difficult to walk in? Better yet, why is it difficult to activate? These questions plagued my mind for many days and many nights.

As I began to ponder and study this subject I became more aware of the importance of purpose, not just for the organized church, but also for the life of every individual. This includes those in the church and those who are not.

I began to realize the importance of purpose in my own life. It was purpose that drastically changed my life. I found out that purpose is what gave meaning to my life. Prior to finding purpose I simply existed. I had routines that I repeated day in and day out. I would go to work, church and home. This routine would go on for days, months and even years. That is, until purpose showed up. Purpose not only affected what I did but how I felt. Without purpose I found myself constantly discouraged, oppressed, and almost depressed. Without purpose I found myself engaging in petty situations and foolishness. I was going nowhere. I simply existed.

Walking in purpose is what we all need to be doing. Failure to walk in purpose will cause us to operate or activate those perceptions, behaviors and habits that snuff out and destroy what God placed on the inside of us, thus messing up our lives. Even Jesus, the Messiah Himself walked in purpose. He, being God, knew beforehand what His purpose was. Jesus' purpose was revealed to man long before He arrived. Matthew 1:21 says, "**And she shall bring forth a son, and thou shalt call his name Jesus; for he shall save his people from their sins.**" There is revelation regarding Jesus and His purpose in the Old Testament. "**Therefore the Lord Himself will give you a sign: Behold, a virgin shall conceive and bear a Son, and shall call His name Immanuel**" (The Immanuel Prophecy found in Isaiah 7:14). His purpose was to come forth at an appointed time. Galations 4, verses 4 and 5 says, "*But when the fullness of the time had come, God sent forth His Son, born of a woman, born under the law, (5) to redeem those who were under the law, that we might receive the adoption as sons.*"

However, it took more than just "knowing about" His purpose. Jesus had to **fulfill** His purpose. In order for His purpose to be fulfilled He had to walk in it. Dying on the cross so that man would be redeemed and spared from eternal destruction and conquering death was His divine appointment (purpose) and destiny. But we must remember Jesus went through it as a human! He ate, slept, felt, cried, etc. just as humans do. He could have chosen to not go through with it. He is God. But glory to God, He fulfilled His purpose! If Jesus had not fulfilled His purpose there would be no way for us to find our purpose. Why? We would be without clue regarding purpose or anything else because we would be on our way to hell!

God **never** does anything haphazardly or without a plan. It has been said that everything that God does and creates is for a reason. If we are to accept this statement as truth, then we must believe that when God created you and me He had something (purpose) in mind, regardless of how we got here. Also, because He created us with a purpose in mind, He has placed within us all that we need to fulfill and carry out this purpose. However, it is up to us to step into this purpose. You see, even though He has given us the ability to carry out His purpose, He has also given us choices concerning it. We have the choice to either fulfill or not fulfill our purpose **and** for whom we will use the abilities God gave us - (God or Satan). God never violates our will.

Allow me to explain. There are many people, both saved and unsaved, who are doing and using what God placed inside of them to do. They are also reaping the benefits of using what was given to them despite their spiritual convictions or lack thereof.

How? Let me explain this quickly. Purpose is a principle. Principles are set in motion to work despite who operates in it. One example of a principle is gravity, which in layman's term states, "What goes up must come down." The law of gravity does not apply to certain people and not to others. No matter what you throw up, as long as it is heavier than air, it will come back down. This principle was established from the foundation of the world. The Bible explains the principle of sowing and reaping. Second Corinthians 9:6 says, "**He who sows sparingly will also reap sparingly and he who sows bountifully will also reap bountifully.**" I have seen many "church folks" discouraged and confused because they have tried to figure out how those who are not Christians are blessed financially. Many of the people that I know who are not Christians and are financially blessed are the type of people who have a heart to give. Many of the well-known millionaires give generously to various organizations and charities. They **sow** bountifully so they **reap** bountifully. This principle does not apply for one group and not the other. It applies to everyone. Just like gravity, it works for everyone. Look for yourself. The scriptures do not say that this is just for believers. The scripture indicates those benefits that are strictly for believers by saying statements such as "to those who believe" (i.e. John 3:16; Mark 16:15-17; Romans 4:23-25; Romans 10:9). It is the same with the principle of purpose. There are benefits, just like with sowing and reaping, when we activate what God has placed inside of us to do. Look at many of the "secular" musicians, singers, and dancers. It is obvious that those gifts came from God. As a matter of fact, the majority of them started in the Church! However, they *chose* to use it in a manner that does not bring glory to God. This is where we get confused. Our purpose is not **divine purpose** unless it brings glory and honor to God. This is why these same people, even though they are using what is inside of them, end up on drugs, alcohol, bad relationships, abuse, etc. They become imprisoned and a slave to those things. They soon realize that something is missing. They try to fill the void that only God can fill. So, let's make it clear. A person might be using the abilities that God has placed in them for their purpose. However, if it is not used for the purpose that God intended through Christ Jesus, and does not glorify God, their lives will end up being unfulfilled (something missing) and their spirit will be eternally destroyed. (Read Matthew 13:24-30, and 36-43).

Even when God created Lucifer (yes, He created him), He created him for a specific purpose. In Ezekial 28:11-19, scholars and commentators believe that this passage of scripture describes Lucifer. It says, "**Moreover the word of the Lord came to me, saying (12) Son of man, take up a lamentation for the king of Tyre, and say to him, Thus says the Lord God: You were the seal of perfection, full of wisdom and perfect in beauty, (13)**

You were in Eden, the garden of God; Every precious stone was your covering. The sardius, topaz, and diamond, beryl, onyx, and jasper, sapphire, turquoise, and emerald with gold. The workmanship of your timbrels and pipes was prepared for you on the day you were created. (14) You were the anointed cherub who covers; I established you; You were on the holy mountain of God; You walked back and forth in the midst of fiery stones. (15) You were perfect in your ways from the day you were created, Till iniquity was found in you. (16) By the abundance of your trading You became filled with violence within, And you sinned; Therefore I cast you as a profane thing Out of the mountain of God; And I destroyed you, O covering cherub, From the midst of the fiery stones. (17) Your heart was lifted up because of your beauty; You corrupted your wisdom for the sake of your splendor I cast you to the ground, I laid you before kings, That they might gaze at you. (18) You defiled your sanctuaries by the multitude of your iniquities, By the iniquity of your trading; Therefore I brought fire from your midst; It devoured you; And I turned you to ashes upon the earth in the sight of all who saw you. (19) All who knew you among the peoples are astonished at you; You have become a horror, And shall be no more forever. (New King James Version).** When reading this passage you will discover God's desired purpose for creating Lucifer and a description of what He placed within him (musical instruments, beauty, anointing). We all know the story of Lucifer and how he was the angel created for worship. He was a true worshipper both inside and outside. Lucifer became full of himself and felt that he deserved the honor given to God. Lucifer decided to do his own thing. This decision led him (and still is leading him) to an end of eternal destruction and doom. Perhaps, if Satan had chosen to continue in the way that God had purposed for him, the outcome would be a lot different.

So, what happens if we don't find our purpose? How will it affect our lives? Will it affect our children and other people in our lives? As you will find out in the upcoming chapters, purpose, or the lack of it, affects the individual and so much more.

If purpose is this important for our lives then why is it so difficult to go forth? There are people who know exactly what God wants them to do but are having a difficult time getting started. If this is you, then this is most definitely the book for you. There are numerous materials and books that address the topic of purpose. We have been very informed regarding its importance. Many great preachers, teachers and evangelist have shared from the Word of God and have given us scriptural references for purpose. However, even with all of this information many of us are stuck in the first stage of purpose. Something (or someone) is hindering us from moving forward. These hindrances become the very thing that kills purpose in the lives of many people.

Are you ready to move forward in purpose? If you feel that you are at a dead-end and you want a way out, then you are ready to go forth in your purpose. If you feel as if your life has no meaning and you are tired of simply existing by doing the same things the same way year after year, then you are ready to go forth in your purpose. If you are tired of putting off doing what you believe God has told you to do, for whatever reason, you are ready to go forth in your purpose. If you feel a void or something missing, then you are ready to go forth in your purpose.

Lastly, there are those who are confused about what they should be doing. They are feeling unsure and doubting what they believe God has purposed for them to do. Others are scared to move forward because of past failures and mistakes. These people are constantly around others who enjoy being reminded of the past. Many are scared to move forward because of being intimidated by others. Well, get ready to shout because your day of emancipation has come! You must remember that God **"has not given us a spirit of fear but of power and of love and of a sound mind"** (2 Timothy 1:7).

As you get ready to open the pages of this book, get ready to move ahead in your purpose. Get ready to break those demons of confusion, procrastination, fear, intimidation and doubt. Get ready to become free by destroying all those things that work to kill God's plan for your life. Once you are freed, you will have the authority and power to loose others into their purpose and destiny.

CHAPTER ONE

FINDING THE ROAD TO PURPOSE

(Knowing Where You Are Going)

Many of us spend a lot of time trying to figure out what we should be doing with our lives. After spending years, time, physical energy and money, we all come to a point of reflection. For some, it is the years close to when they realize that "the biological clock is ticking" and will not "tick" forever. For others it is the time during the "change of life" or what is called the "mid-life crisis". There are those who begin reflecting on all that they have done and have become disappointed when they realize what they have been doing no longer works or satisfies. Something is missing.

When I passed the wonderful age of 35 a few years ago I was feeling like an unfulfilled woman. Yes, I had (and still have) a wonderful husband, beautiful children, a career, and a few engagements to sing or preach, but yet, something was still missing. I was constantly doing a lot of things but somewhere I was like the Israelites in the wilderness - moving but going nowhere. I found myself thinking a lot about death because somewhere inside I was dying. One day while in prayer, I began to ask God these questions. Why was I born? Why am I here?

What is missing in my life? Where am I going? Why am I feeling this way? The answer was clear. My life was missing purpose.

WHAT IS PURPOSE

Second Timothy 1:9 says, "**(God) who hath saved us, and called us with an holy calling, not according to our works, but according to his own purpose and grace, which was given us in Christ Jesus before the world began.**

This passage of scripture informs us that before the world began, God called us with a holy calling according to His own purpose and grace. This is called a **predestined purpose**.

According to Webster's Dictionary, the word purpose means "intention or resolution". It is further defined as "the intended usage for an object and/or person". Determination (act of deciding definitely and firmly) is also used to define purpose. Many people use the words purpose and destiny interchangeably. Both words, in a spiritual sense, could mean the same. For example a person's destiny **should** be their purpose. However, there are times, for example in a secular sense of this word, when there is a profound difference between the two. In a secular sense, whatever a person's destiny is may not necessarily be their purpose. For example let's say that God's divine purpose for someone is for him or her to minister to the homeless. What happens if the person **chooses** not to do this? What if the person, for some reason, were turned off by "religion" and decided to "live life to the fullest" by partying and drinking whenever he/she could? That person could be *destined* for a life of destruction based on how he/she lived unless he/she *chooses* to repent and return to God. How this person *chooses* to live will map out where he/she is headed. With others who are doing things that don't line up with what God purposed for them, their destiny might not be as destructive as a person who lives a life of sin, however it will still be missing something.

Divine purpose, as used in scripture, is seen as God's **predestined** intention for a person. The word "predestined" (root word destine) means that it was determined long before it was brought to pass. **Destiny** means "to designate, assign or dedicate *in advance*; to direct, devise or set apart (sanctify) for a specific purpose or place" (Revell's Bible Dictionary). Therefore, when we speak of God's purpose for our lives we are referring to what He had determined in advance (before our conception) for us to do. What is YOUR purpose?

When trying to understand divine purpose the best place to go would be the Word of God. The one thing I find amazing about us church going folk is that we read stories regarding these great men and women of the Bible, and we get excited about what God did in their lives back then. But, do we ever realize that the great things that God did in the lives of those great prophets, teachers, preachers and evangelist, He desires to do the same in our lives today?

There is one book of the Bible that illustrates a detailed and distinct example of purpose. This is the book of Jeremiah. Just as God had a purpose for Jeremiah, He has one for you and me today. What is YOUR purpose?

The first few verses of the book of Jeremiah begin by informing us of the geneology of Jeremiah. In chapter one, verse four; Jeremiah is informed of God's plan for his life. Verse (4) says, "**Then the word of the Lord came unto me, saying, (5) Before I formed thee in the belly I knew thee; and before thou camest forth out of the womb I sanctified thee, and I ordained thee a prophet unto the nations. (6) Then said I, Ah Lord God! Behold, I cannot speak; for I am a child. (7) But the Lord said unto me, Say not, I am a child; for thou shalt go to all that I shall send thee, and whatsoever I command thee thou shalt speak. (8) Be not afraid of their faces: for I am with thee to deliver thee, saith the Lord. (9) Then the Lord put forth his hand, and touched my mouth. And the Lord said unto me, Behold I have put my words in thy mouth. (10) See, I have this day set thee over the nations and over the kingdoms, to root out, and to pull down, and to destroy and to throw down, to build and to plant.** In verse 17, it continues, **(17) Thou therefore gird up thy loins, and arise, and speak unto them all that I** command thee; be not dismayed at their faces, lest I confound thee before them. (18) For, behold I have made thee this day a defenced city and an iron pillar, and brasen walls against the whole land, against the kings of Judah, against the princes thereof, against the priests thereof, and against the people of the land. (19) And they shall fight against thee; but they shall not prevail against thee; for I am with thee, saith the Lord, to deliver thee.**

In verse four the Lord informs Jeremiah that **before** he was formed in the womb of his mother he had a **(predestined)** purpose for his life. In other words, God determined beforehand what He wanted to do with Jeremiah's life. He told Jeremiah that he **sanctified** (set him apart) and **ordained** (established) him to be a prophet to the nations.

Now, before going on, it is important to understand that predestined purpose is not only for Jeremiah and those of biblical times. This cannot be said enough! Romans 8:28-30, a very familiar passage of scripture, states, **"And we know that all things work together for good to them that love God, to them who are the called according to His purpose. (29) For whom He did foreknow He also did predestinate to be conformed to the image of His Son, that he might be the firstborn among many brethren.** We use this scripture to encourage each other during those times of trials and tribulation. However, it is in verse 30 where we learn of God's intentions for our lives. It says, **"Moreover whom He did predestinate, them he also called and whom he called, them He also justified and whom He justified, them He also glorified.** What does this mean? God has a pre-determined, pre-planned purpose for all of us, just as He did with Jeremiah. These pre-planned purposes are those callings that He has placed within us before we were conceived. It goes on to say that those He calls He **justifies** (deem as righteous) and those he justifies He **glorifies** (brings honor to). Our purposes were given **by** Him to be used **for** Him. Therefore, we don't need the praises of men because God will bring the honor to us.

Some have asked the question, "When or where does purpose begin?" I am going to quote my husband Anthony to answer this question. "Purpose is a part of God's overall plan, therefore it is eternal. Because it is eternal, it has no beginning or ending. It will always exist." Now, God has a predestined purpose for everyone and everything. Our individual purposes fit into God's overall plan. It is up to us to seek it. It is also up to us to choose whom we do it for. To not do it for God is, by default, doing it for Satan. We sit in the church week after week and every time someone has to remind us that we need to worship God. But the truth is that when we as creations of God, fulfill our divine purpose (as He commanded) that is when we bring glory, honor and worship to God. We will talk more on this later on.

Once we grasp the concept that God created us with a specific purpose (or calling) in mind the next question we all need to ask ourselves is what exactly does God want with me? This is usually the first area of struggle once we realize that there is a purpose. Once we accept the concept of divine purpose many of us come to a complete halt because we now need to know exactly what God wants with us. Where do we begin?

As I reflect back on my life, I have come to realize that many of the things I did years ago flow directly into what I am doing now. How? Truthfully, I do not know. The transition from one to the other seems to happen naturally. During my childhood I was deeply into playing the piano, singing, and composing music. The majority of my singing was done in church. Later on, I became Minister of Music for a Baptist church and the founder/executive director of two community choirs. As I ventured out into these ministries, within me grew a desire to do more. Within me grew a desire to know more about God and myself. I needed a deeper relationship with the Lord. As my relationship with the Lord grew, I become more fascinated with the Word. The more fascinated I became with the Word the more I learned about myself and about God's plans for my life. I felt God calling me to the ministry however; I began to ask, "How could God use such a messed up person like me?" As a choir director and musician I no longer found (only) singing satisfying. What was missing? Little by little, during concerts or while singing a solo, I would feel a strong urge and I would end up doing more preaching than singing! As my relationship with the Lord grew His voice became clear. Eventually, there arose within me a burden for souls being saved. God began instructing me to spend more time leading people to Christ and less time getting them to sing well! It was difficult because God was requiring me to tend to the spiritual needs of a "come as you are" choir. However, when I OBEYED **His command**, it moved me to the next level of purpose. Obeying the Lord enabled me to transcend from one level to the next and it happened without my own assistance. I did not have to force it; it happened naturally.

Purpose does not always mean a change in **what** one does but **how** one does what they do. When talking to various people who are activated in their purposes, many of them are doing what they have always been doing, but on a higher level. It may be in the same area but its not done the same way. For example, there are people that I know who have always been good with children. You could always find the young people at their house. As their relationship with the Lord grew, He began to do more with them. God has moved many of them into Children and Youth Ministries. Many of them are over the youth at their churches, running after school programs, or holding monthly youth rap sessions. There are others who started off doing one thing and it ended up being a stepping-stone to what they are doing today. For example, many Pastors and Evangelists began as singers, musicians, and choir directors. Many still have the ability to minister in music. However, they are now more activated in the "preaching" ministry. There are others whose initial activity served as a training ground to further purpose in their lives. For example, my husband worked years as a church bookkeeper. He believed this was what God had called him to do. A few years later, he began a home-based business. Soon after, he was blessed with an office in the community. Ever since he's been in the office he's had numerous opportunities to minister and witness to many people.

As we look in the scriptures we can find examples of a person's initial activity that acted as a training ground for their future purpose. Do you remember David? Everyone tells, with avid enthusiasm, the story of David and Goliath. However, it was the activities of David's past, which prepared him for his future fight with Goliath. Now, I feel that it is important to remind you that this fight with Goliath was not David's final destination on his road to purpose however, it played an important factor in preparing him for what God had for him to do. As we all know, David later became one of the greatest Kings.

David's purpose was foretold long before he came on the scene. First Samuel, verse 13:14 says, "**But now thy kingdom shall not continue; the Lord hath sought him a man after his** own heart, and the Lord hath commanded him to be captain over his people, because thou hast not kept that which the Lord commanded thee.** Here, Samuel was speaking to Saul who was the king at that time. Saul was being rebuked for being disobedient. However, Samuel was informing him that God had someone in mind that was going to be the king. Now, David's name was not mentioned here, but as you will see later, Samuel was referring to David. In First Samuel 16:1. It says, "**And the Lord said unto Samuel, How long wilt thou mourn for Saul, seeing I have rejected him from reigning over Israel? Fill thine horn with oil, and go, I will send thee to Jesse the Bethlehemite: for I have provided me a king among his sons.** This is another statement establishing a pre-determined, pre-planned purpose. However, there is still no mentioning of David. All we know is that God already had someone, a man after His own heart, to rule over His people. This man was one of Jesse's sons.

In 1 Samuel 16:11 we learn of David's occupation as a sheepherder. Samuel sent for David who was not among the sons who came with Jesse. Chapter 16:12-13 says, "**And he sent, and brought him in. Now he was ruddy, and withal of a beautiful countenance, and goodly to look to. And the Lord said, Arise, anoint him; for this is he. (13) Then Samuel took the horn of oil, and anointed him in the midst of his brethren; and the**

spirit of the Lord came upon David from that day forward. So Samuel rose up, and went to Ramah. As you read on you find that David walked in his anointing from that day forward. This was the beginning of David moving towards greatness.

In Chapter 17 you will find the popular story of the battle between David and Goliath. Now, we will not go into details regarding the fight between David and Goliath. However it is important to focus on a few key verses.

In 1 Samuel 17:18 David, being too young, was not allowed to fight. His father sent him to bring food to his older brothers and the Captain, who were fighting the Phillistines. As you continue on to verse 26, you will find David inquiring about Goliath. In verse 29 we find where David recognizes a cause. Family and friends tried to discourage him but were unsuccessful. In verse 32, David's purpose is revealed. He says," **Let no man's heart fail because of him; thy servant will go and fight with this Phillistine."** In other words, he realized that he was the one who was divinely appointed to take Goliath out! In verse 33, Saul tries to discourage David by highlighting an obvious factor (David's age), which made no difference to David. David had a purpose and even though he was considered to be inexperienced (youth) he referred back to his experience as a sheepherder, which qualified him for the task at hand. He was determined to go through with this fight. This determination is seen in verses 34 through 37.

"And David said unto Saul, Thy servant kept his father's sheep, and there came a lion, and a bear, and took a lamb out of the flock. (35) And I went out after him, and smote him, and delivered it out of his mouth; and when he arose against me, I caught him by his beard, and smote him, and slew him. (36) Thy servant slew both the lion and the bear, and this uncircumcised Phillistine shall be as one of them, seeing he hath defied the armies of the living God. (37) David said, moreover, The Lord that delivered me out of the paw of the lion, and out of the paw of the bear, he will deliver me out of the hand of this Phillistine. And Saul said unto David, Go, and the Lord be with thee. You must get this. It was his life as a sheepherder, which acted as a training ground to fight this giant. David felt very equipped to fight Goliath because of his experience as a sheepherder. He fought with the tools he used to protect the sheep. The years David was protecting the sheep was an important time for him. What would have happened to David if he chose not to remain in this position as a sheepherder? What am I saying? Never underestimate what you may be doing now? Whatever you find yourself doing now may be the training ground for what you could be doing later on. I am pretty sure that David, the sheepherder, never thought he would one day be David the king! Most people, in David's shoes, would have most likely disregarded their shepherding occupation!

Hopefully, at this point you desire to get started. Or, perhaps you are currently doing something and you need direction on where to go or what to do next. I used to hear people say, "If you want to know what something is used for, then contact the people or person who made it." This principle holds true for finding our purposes. Ephesians 2:10 says, "**For we are his workmanship, created in Christ Jesus unto good works, which God hath before ordained that we should walk in them.**" If you want to know what your purpose is or what to do next then it is time for you to contact your creator.

If we REALLY understand that God created everything with a specific purpose, then we should understand the danger of doing something we were not made for. Look at what happens to society when it takes the things that were created for one purpose and use them for another. God placed many of the plants on this earth for maintaining our physical health but in some cases they are used for something else. What do we have? People destroying themselves, drug abuse, drug overdoses, drug addictions and many times drug-related crimes.

It is important to know that a life that serves no purpose displeases God. I am reminded of the parable of the fig tree and how it relates to "religion." Matthew 21:18-19 says, "**Now in the morning as He returned to the city, He was hungry. And seeing a fig tree by the road He came to it and found nothing**

on it but leaves and said to it, "Let no fruit grow on you ever again." Immediately the fig tree withered away." Fig trees were created by God to bring forth fruit and not just leaves. Religion (not relationship) teaches us to bring forth leaves with no fruit. We may LOOK like the real thing but that does not matter. If we don't produce what God has purposed, we are really of no use to Him.

  It is important to understand the part that relationship plays in your purpose. In order for David to be a man after God's own heart he had to be in relationship with Him. "Being a man after God's own heart" implies that David knew what moved and touched God. David was concerned about the things that concerned God. In order to know what concerned God, David had to be one who was constantly in touch with Him. How can one find his or her purpose if they are disconnected from the One who is responsible for creating them and placing this (purpose) within them. David communicated with God on a daily basis. If communicating with Him is difficult then it is time to work on establishing a relationship with Him. Talking with the Lord will give you access to Him whenever and wherever you need Him. The more you open yourself up to Him the clearer **PURPOSE** and what to do next becomes. This is the first step to finding your purpose and moving on to whatever the Lord has next for your life.

CHAPTER TWO

OBEDIENCE

(DOING WHAT YOU ARE TOLD)

After establishing a relationship with the Lord, the next step involves **listening** to what He says and then **doing** as He commands. This is called **obedience**. Obedience, according to the Hebrews and Greek, means, "to hear" (Revell's Bible Dictionary). Further study of this word shows that obedience involves "relationship". The hearer who responds to the expressed will of another is in some form of relationship with the subject. The one who is in authority knows personally the one receiving instruction. When it comes to God, only those who are in relationship with Him are willing to obey Him. We willingly obey because He knows our purpose and will guide us according to that for which He created us. Those who say that they are in right relationship with the Lord feel that they love Him. However, the scripture says, **"if we love Him we would keep His commandments"** (John 14:15). This requires obeying and doing whatever He commands.

How far are you willing to go for the sake of your purpose? Are you willing to do whatever God asks, whenever He asks? Or, is there a limit to your obedience? Are you willing to go all the way? Let me give you a biblical example.

God, after creating the world, looked at mankind, whom He created, and later saw the wickedness in them. God realized that He had to destroy them (Genesis 6:5-7).

Verse 8 says, "**But Noah found grace in the eyes of the Lord.**" This is the first indication that God had a plan for Noah. There were others on the earth but out of all the other people God could have chosen, he chose Noah. Remember that God does not do anything haphazardly. For everything that He creates He has a purpose. For everything that He does, there is a reason and a purpose. Therefore, God must have spared Noah for a reason. Verse nine establishes that Noah had a relationship with God. (9) **These are the generations of Noah; Noah was a just man and perfect in his generations, and Noah walked with God.**" Noah's "walk with God" establishes that he had a relationship with Him. When two people walk together this illustrates that there is a covenant and fellowship between them.

In verses 13-16 you will find God giving specific instructions to Noah regarding what he was to do. As you read on, God informs Noah of the flood and then makes a covenant with Noah and his family. God went on to give Noah further instructions. Noah never questioned why God was requiring him to build this ark. Verse 22 says, "**Thus did Noah; according to**

all that God commanded him, so did he." God gave Noah more and more instructions and each time he did as he was commanded (7:5). I have heard many preachers say how they believed that the people mocked Noah. If the people then were anything like people today, I am certain that he was mocked!

I believe that when Noah was doing all that God had commanded, he was unaware of the part that he played in the bigger picture. He most likely felt that he simply found favor in the eyes of God. Therefore, He was being spared destruction. I tend to believe that Noah was not thinking about *why* God would spare him. He, as with any human being, was probably just happy to be spared. In any case, Noah's obedience was a stepping-stone for his participation in the larger purpose, which is God's overall plan.

In Genesis chapter 9, verse 1; we learn that Noah's purpose involved his sons. We will discuss purpose and lineage later on in chapter seven. This verse also confirms God's intentions for Noah. It says, " **And God blessed Noah and his sons, and said unto them, Be fruitful, and multiply, and replenish the earth."** From Noah's three sons, **"of them was the whole earth overspread" (9:19).** Noah's obedience led him to open the doors not only to his purpose but also to the purposes of his children. Chapter 10 of Genesis tells us of the generations of Noah's grandchildren and their purposes. It says, **"These are the families of the sons of**

Noah, after their generations, in their nations and by these were the nations divided in the earth after the flood." All of this began from the obedience of one man, Noah. He and his wife "were fruitful" and they multiplied. Noah had no limits on what he could do. Despite how it might have looked to others, Noah trusted God and was willing to do whatever He commanded even if he looked stupid! Noah was unaware of God's overall purpose for his life. However, he never once questioned why God had him building the ark. He just listened and obeyed.

From the lineage of Noah comes a man by the name of Abram, who would continue on from Noah's purpose. Abram, later known as Abraham, was a grand son (many greats) of Noah.

Abram was given instructions and told his purpose for his life at the same time. Genesis 12:1-3 says, "**Now the Lord had said unto Abram, Get thee out of thy country, and from thy kindred, and from thy father's house, unto a land that I will show thee: (2) And I will make of thee a great nation, and I will bless thee, and make thy name great; and thou shalt be a blessing. (3) And I will bless them that bless thee, and curse him that curseth thee; and in thee shall all families of the earth be blessed**." Verses 4 and 5 inform us that Abram obeyed. He was told to take his family and possessions and move. Now, if you look at verse one, God told Abram that He would "show" him a land. In other words, Abram did not know where he was going.

He just went. Throughout Abram's journey the Lord reminded him of His intentions (purpose) for his life (10:7). Abram remained obedient despite the famine in the land.

In Chapter 13, you will find Abram, now a wealthy man, parting ways with his nephew. Again, the Lord reminds Abram of his purpose. In verse 15-16 He says, **"For all the land which thou seest; to thee will I give it, and to thy seed forever. (16) And I will make thy seed as the dust of the earth; so that if a man can number the dust of the earth, then shall thy seed also be numbered."**

In Chapter 15 we see the "human nature" of Abram. God told him that from his seed he would bring forth a great nation. Abram, having a barren wife, was inquiring about when he would have a child. Again God reminds Abram of the promise that would be fulfilled in his purpose. Abraham **"believed in the Lord; and he counted it to him for righteousness"** (Verse 6). God continued to give Abram instructions and he continued to be obedient to what He said. Abram was so protective about God's instructions to him that **"when the fowls came down upon the carcasses, Abram drove them away" (15:11).**

Chapter 16 of Genesis helps me understand why God, if He chooses, would not reveal everything to us all at once. Abram knew what God desired of him. However, it was not happening quickly enough for him. Therefore, Abram and his wife Sarai decided to take matters into their own hands. God had promised that they would conceive a child. It was taking too long. Therefore, if **Sarai** could not conceive this promised child, then they would find a way to **make** it happen. Sarai told Abram to go to her servant Hagar and she would conceive a son **for** them. This act ended up backfiring within their house (16:4). However, God being merciful did not lift or take away the purpose of Abram. Just as He promised, despite what it looked like, Sarah conceived (Chapter 21).

Let me add here. Many of us have made or continue to make this mistake. Once we gain an understanding about what God desire for us to do, we go and try to **make** it happen according to our own understanding. We experience setbacks because we were unable to wait on the Lord. Just like with Sarai and Abram, we end up hurting ourselves.

ABRAHAM continued to be obedient. If you continue to read throughout Genesis, you will find that this purpose, which began with Noah, continues throughout the generations. If you read carefully you will see that obedience was the major prerequisite for moving forward in purpose.

The area of obedience was where I used to struggle. Once I established my relationship with the Lord He would give me instructions. These instructions came by way of studying the Word, prayer, and meditation and sometimes through the mouths of men and women of God. The more I learned about God the more I learned about and understood His purpose for my life. At first, whatever I believed God was telling me to do I did without any questions. But somewhere that began to change.

I remember attending various services and revivals, and someone would come up to me and tell me what God was going to do in my life. Was this new information to me? No. He had told me when I prayed, meditated and studied. Truthfully, I had heard it so many times that I was beginning to become immune to hearing it. What do I mean? At first, I would jump up and down, excited about how God was going to use me. But as the years passed it seemed as if nothing was happening. As a matter of fact, there was nothing but drama and hardship in my life. Where were the blessings that were prophesied to me? I began to question God. Just like Abram, I looked at my current circumstances and situations and wanted to know **how and when** God planned to carry this out. To me, God was taking too long. Picture that! I began to ask, was I not doing what He wanted me to do? This affected my trust level and in return I began to question the purpose God had for me. You see, unlike Noah and Abram, I "obeyed" God as long as what He was asking of me made sense to me.

Please, allow me to be transparent. When I first acknowledged my call to the ministry, God had shown me that I was called to an international ministry. He told me, through various instruments, that He was going to use me to restore, edify and free His people all over the world with the Word of God. All I had to do was to do whatever He asked me to do.

In the first few years of ministry I was extremely excited. If God had told me to break dance in the middle of the road, I would have done it! I was just that eager and excited about the things of God. However, as years passed I realized that I was in the same place, around the same people and doing the same thing the same way! Not much had changed. What was wrong?

One day God spoke to my husband and me about moving. We knew it was time for us to move. We obeyed the voice of God and moved. This was difficult for me because I had never been away from home and we were attached to the people in the ministry choir that we started seven years earlier. Yet, we knew it was time to move. As I began to "analyze the situation" I felt that moving made sense! Moving, as I had perceived, meant another level of purpose. I was excited. Look at how God was moving in my life! Little did I know this excitement was short-lived. Things had settled down in my new environment and it seemed like I was doing the same thing as I was doing in my previous environment. However, as I reflect back there were numerous things that the Lord wanted me to learn but I was too busy trying to figure Him out! I spent a lot of time trying to *make* things happen (just like

Sarai and Abraham) only to make matters worse. During the first eight months I sat still. I went to work, home and church. At church, I did absolutely nothing. Well, then again I was doing something - complaining. I criticized everything and had ideas of how "those things" could be fixed. Here God showed me two things: 1) I was part of the problem because I had the solution but was too full of myself to help: 2) He had placed me there to work and learn for a period of time.

Eventually, it was time to move again. To me, this did not make any sense. I did not feel that this was "of God" so I tried to do everything to stay. Life became a kind of Hell! Doors began closing all over the place. But I will never forget one Sunday service at the church I was attending. On this particular Sunday the power of God was so strong. I went to the altar and gave everything up! I was tired and did not care anymore. I told God to do whatever He had to do. I don't remember if I was tired of fighting or if I was willingly submitted to what God wanted. Whichever one it was, I gave it to Him. Guess what? That is what He was waiting for! God had been tying to get my attention for the longest. However, I was so bent on doing it my own way. Somewhere along the way I stopped listening for the voice of God. I realized that it was better for me to obey God.

I still have not reached the level that God said I would, but I am using this time to work on being obedient. One act of obedience for me was writing this book. Now, to me, it did not make "sense" to write a book when no one knows who I am. But, I immediately put that thought under subjection! As the young people say "I had to check it!" The Bible informs us that **"His thoughts are not our thoughts nor is His ways our ways."** All I needed to do was obey Him. It was time for me to trust in the Lord with all my heart and lean not to my own understandings. I needed to acknowledge Him in all my ways and then have faith that He would direct my path (Proverbs 3:5-6).

      What has God asked you to do that you continue to ignore? Do you find yourself being led to do something but somehow you talk yourself out of it? Are you guilty of complaining about what's wrong with everything (husband, wife, kids, job, church etc.)? Perhaps you know someone who complains ALL THE TIME; nothing is ever right. If you have answered yes to these questions then you may need to check how obedient you are to God. If you know someone or are in relationship with someone like this, you need to allow God to take control of that situation or before you know it, you will begin to complain. If you are ready to be obedient to whatever God commands you to do, just make a decision and ***do it!*** Obey the voice of the Lord. Repent to the Lord and ask Him to forgive you for being disobedient. Do it right now. You have nothing to fear because the Word says that when we sin, **"He is faithful and just to forgive"**(1 John 1:9).

So far we have gathered three important factors in stepping out in purpose: 1) Recognize that you HAVE a purpose. 2) Build a relationship with God so you can hear what He says to you. 3) Do what He tells you to do.

Don't waste another second, get started RIGHT NOW!

CHAPTER THREE

SEASONS OF PURPOSE

When we get to the place of walking in obedience, we will see our purpose move from one level to the next. Going from level to level could mean doing the same thing over but on a higher level or doing something completely different. If you follow the lives of many of the great men and women in the Bible you will see that many of the things that they did were done during an appointed time. Each new level represents a new season. I watch famous people and wonder how they got to where they are. I think about the powerful evangelist, ministers, pastors, musicians, singers, soloist and businessmen and wonder what did it cost to get to that level of ministry and business. If we had the chance to speak to these various men and women who are operating in purpose they would inform us that it did not start out this way. They had to go from level to level which means they had to go through seasons of ministries.

The Word declares that everything we do is done during a specific season and time Ecclesiastes 3:1 says, **"to every thing there is a season, and a time to every purpose under the heaven."** In order to grasp the concept of this verse it is important to understand the definition of two words: **seasons** and **time**.

The word **season** refers to "an appointed period." The word **time** has a few definitions. It is defined as a "pre-determined occurrence" and "an opportunity." The Hebrew word used in this text is "Anah, which means to be exercised." If we are to fully understand this verse we would acknowledge that the things we do must be exercised during an appointed time period that was set in motion before hand (pre-determined occurrence) and will occur at the opportune moment.

Even though the examples used in this chapter (3:2-8) are seen as "poetic metaphors" (Wycliffe), the analogies used are clear in illustrating that seasons are vital elements in determining what and when something should be done.

When I look back over my life there were times when I was doing the same thing for a long time. For most of my life I was a choir director and musician. You could always find me teaching songs or playing for someone. This was natural for me to do. When I began to feel the call to the preaching ministry it was such a struggle. As I said before, I had a hard time believing that God would use me in this way. But, that was not the only reason. I had made up in my mind that I was going to be this international Gospel singer, producer, composer, etc. I was going to have this great mass choir and I would be traveling all over this world! Now, God can STILL allow that to happen. At that time, I thought that in order to do one thing, I would have to give up the other.

Needless to say, I had limited not only myself, but I had also limited what God could do through me. How? In my mind, I wanted to do what I wanted. God was not going to violate my will. Remember, God gives us the freedom to choose. This desire to be this world-renowned Gospel artist was something that I wanted to do. But the question remained "What about God?" If the truth is told, I never consulted Him. I was too focused on my own desires. I had assumed that because I was known for my musical abilities I would only be doing music. It never occurred to me that God could use me in both areas. Both could work hand in hand, complementing each other. Where you find preaching, isn't music usually involved? God was ready to strengthen and prepare me for what was coming next in my life. I did not realize that I was in another season of purpose. There were things I did for a short season and then there were things I did for a long season. It is important for you to know, as I had to find out, what season you are in so that you will be operating in and doing the right thing.

When God created you, He did so with a specific purpose in mind (predestination). The purpose in which God desires for you to operate is part of His overall purpose. Remember what we learned about Abram? He went through many seasons. In one season he was journeying to a land that God brought him to. This was the season of obedience. He did not know where God was taking him, but he was willing to do whatever He commanded.

Another season involved faith testing where God fulfills the promise of giving Abram a son and then turns around and tells him to offer the son as a sacrifice. Notice how this season involved what he learned during the first season, obedience. He "obeyed" the command of God but this time he also had to trust in and have faith in Him. God, as always, kept His promise. It did not stop there. There were many more seasons in Abram's life. All of the seasons in Abram's life were necessary for God to bring about the "nations from his seed", with whom He would make a covenant.

Each season of purpose ushered Abram to the next level. After establishing a relationship with God, the next season (level) required Abram's obedience. Just like his grandfather Noah, Abram had become accustomed to doing exactly as God commanded. This obedience strengthened Abram's faith in the Lord. No matter what God told him to do, Abram trusted God. Let's be real about something. What would you do if God told you to kill one of your children or someone else that you love? No, I am not telling you to go and kill your children! Today if you hear a voice telling you to kill your child, then you need to rebuke the devil! What you need to see is the principle of this story. Through the story of Abram's willingness to sacrifice his son we learn that we must trust God in a way that supersedes human comprehension. Abraham was willing to trust God with everything, including that which was most precious to him. We must be willing to have faith and trust God above everything, including that which is most precious to us. In principle, Abram was offering his son back to God. Today, we call this christening. When I read that story I immediately began evaluating my standing with the Lord. I asked myself, do I trust God on this level? Abram's obedience shows us that he had such a trust in God that he was willing to do whatever God commanded. Abram had to believe that if God was going to take away what He gave him, He was going to bless him with something greater. The test of faith during this season prepared him for the tests of faith during the next season. Each test of faith required much more from Abram during each new season, and each season ushered Abram into the next level of purpose. Remember Luke 12:48 tells us that to whom much is given much is required. Each season of purpose brought more blessings and favor to Abram. Even in his old age, Abram (now Abraham) was blessed (Genesis 24:1).

Jesus Himself operated in season. He first became human. We know He was born (Matthew 1:25) and worked as a carpenter (Mark 6:3). Then there was the season of His public ministry of preaching, teaching and performing miracles (Read all of the Gospels). Later, He experienced the seasons of opposition. He experienced being slandered and threatened. During this season there were those who tried to discredit Him (Matthew 12:22-37). Then there were the seasons of His crucifixion, death. Then the risen Christ (John 19:17-42; 20). All of these seasons were part of God's purpose for Jesus. He now reigns in heaven to be worshipped by those who believe.

How many times have you heard this question, "Are you ready to go to the next level?" No matter what conference, revival or church service you've attended, you could hear the people shout with such excitement that they were "ready to go to the next level." I was one of the main ones shouting and screaming! I would scream so hard until I made myself hoarse. I remember saying that statement many times over and over. However, the truth is that I was only *saying* it because nothing was happening in my life at that time! I was tired of the way that I was living. The very inside of my soul was tapped out! I was financially struggling and life was extremely stressful. So, a *new level*, to me, meant "Get me away from these issues and problems." The more I studied the Word the more I understood that going to the next level" meant that I acknowledge that my current season is over and I am now listening for the voice of God to instruct me on what to do next. I needed to get to the point where obedience became innate whenever God spoke. My opinions should no longer matter. I also had to understand that the next level could mean doing what I did before with some modification and changes or venturing out into something totally different or brand new. I now understand that going to the next level uses elements from the previous season as a training ground, just as it did for Abram and David. In order for me to go to the next level I had to **let go** of some things and **move on**. This was one of the hardest things for many of us to do. We are sometimes scared to leave what is familiar. I, like many of you, was complacent where I was. I remember vividly the time when I felt a struggle going on inside of me. Where I was, no longer worked. However, during this time I mistook this struggle as "the devil being busy" when all along it was God trying to get me to move! Listen, it is very easy to become discouraged, especially during a very trying and difficult season. Some of you reading this book have been in a long season, and it may appear that you can't endure the struggles, trials, and tribulations that come with this season. God knows that I can relate to this. As I am writing I am reminded of the times in which the burdens of a season seemed too much to bear. I can remember one particular season of financial hardship, personal struggles and uncertainty regarding what God wanted and where He was taking me. Many prophesied that my breakthrough was coming soon! Five years had past and my breakthrough seemed to be nowhere in sight. One day I knelt before God and told Him that I was discouraged, tired and finished! I could not go on until I got an answer. I opened up to Romans Chapter 5 and just started reading. The first five verses spoke to my spirit. It said this: **"Therefore having been justified by faith, we have peace with God through our Lord Jesus**

Christ, through whom also we have access by faith into this grace in which we stand, and rejoice in hope of the glory of God. And not only that, but we also glory in tribulations, knowing that tribulation produces perseverance and perseverance, character and character, hope. Now hope does not disappoint, because the love of God has been poured out in our hearts by the Holy Spirit who was given to us." I stopped after the fifth verse and wept. I wanted to go to the next level (season) but the training process was not complete! God was building within me endurance, character and strengthening my faith, which would give me hope. I felt I was not ready! He was putting me through what was necessary if I was to make it at the next level (season). How I was operating at that time was not going to work for the next level. This is the mistake that we make in our lives. Instead of using the principles learned in a previous season, we take methods that we used during one season and try to use them during another. Then we wonder why we are unsuccessful.

It is so important to see and hear what God is doing and saying in this hour and in this season of your life. It is important not just to hear what God is saying but be willing to **do** whatever He asks. Once we realize that our purpose operates in seasons, we will understand that what we did in 1994 may not work in 2004.

CHAPTER FOUR

PURPOSE AND PEOPLE PLEASING

So far we have learned that we must first build a relationship with God, listen to what He tells us to do and then obey. Our purposes are broken up into seasons. Understanding seasons is what motivates us to move to the next level of purpose in our lives.

One of the most difficult decisions about purpose come with determining whether or not what we are doing is really the purpose of God or the purpose that people have put into us. It is amazing how much power we allow people to have over our lives. Many times, being influenced by people dictates what a person will or will not do. There are people who feel God is telling them to do something. However, they are easily detoured because they feel others may not accept or like what they would be doing. Others sit in the pews week after week waiting for someone to tell them what to do and when to move. If they have the chance to do something, then they want someone to tell them how to do it. These people are too concerned with how other people think or feel.

This was one of the problems that Abram and Sarai had. Genesis 16:2-4 says, "**And Sarai said unto Abram, Behold now,**

the Lord hath restrained me from bearing; I pray thee, go in unto my maid; it may be that I may obtain children by her, And Abram hearkened to the voice of Sarai. (3) And Sarai Abram's wife took Hagar her maid the Egyptian, after Abram had dwelt ten years in the land of Canaan and gave her to her husband Abram to be his wife. (4) And he went in unto Hagar, and she conceived; and which she saw that she had conceived, her mistress was despised in her eyes. Now, you may be thinking that Sarai was acting just like any woman would. This may be so. However, in their custom, "to be childless was a calamity and a disgrace for any Hebrew wife" (Wycliffe Commentary). In order to not look and feel disgraced among her people, Sarai decided to disregard the divine promise given by God and take matters into her own hands. Sarai justified her act by reminding Abram that it was the Lord who made her barren. Apparently to Sarai, she had to find another way.

If most of us were to tell the truth we would acknowledge that many times we don't know what God wants because we spend too much time being concerned with how others think or feel. This is called **people pleasing**. People-pleasing refers to a person obsessed with doing what another person wants him/her to do. Usually, the person who is "doing the pleasing", does not benefit as much (or not at all) as the person he/she is trying to please. Many times the people being pleased are only looking out for themselves. This could also be defined as what we call peer pressure. I did not realize how this affected my purpose and destiny until I had the opportunity to preach for a youth conference on the topic of "Overcoming Peer Pressure, Stress, Struggles and Temptations."

Prior to studying and preparing for the conference, I had assumed that **peer pressure** was strictly seen as being a "young person's " problem. Peer pressure refers to a person, usually of the same group or age of another person, influencing what the person does or does not do. Anyone who can be classified as a peer and influences what I do places pressure on me despite my age. In other words, I do what the other person wants in order to please them.

This was another area in which God had to deal with me. Being a musician, wherever I went people expected me to play. I remember vividly one church service where the preacher said, "There is someone here with whom God desires to do more, but whoever it is can't let go of what he or she is doing." I could feel the Spirit of God rise within me. I knew that I needed to be at the altar. I wanted to break away from that organ so badly, but I was expected to keep the altar music going. Besides, what would the people think if I go to the altar? When service was over, I left church feeling disgusted and bound. That was twelve years ago! I felt that I had disappointed God but the power of what was expected of me was too strong. Sounds familiar? This is not only true for musicians but for many areas like ministry, business, etc. This stronghold stands throughout the church from the pulpit to the door. People pleasing!

One place where people pleasing takes place within the Church is one of a very sensitive and controversial matter. Why? It involves people trying to please leadership. You may be saying, "What is wrong with trying to please my leader? Are we not commanded to be obedient to those who have authority over us?" Let me give you an example and then we can clarify a few things.

There is a young woman whom I will call Ladybird. Ladybird attended a very vibrant church. She was the type of person who desired to please God no matter what it took. One day, Ladybird called me because she was confused. She had a situation and did not know what to do. Ladybird began telling me how her leader had told her to do something that she did not feel led to do. Ladybird felt God leading her to do something else. In this Church, not to do what you were told was considered being disobedient, rebellious and disrespectful to leadership. If you stood your ground you were told to leave the church and were ostracized. These commands were not discussed with the person, therefore leaving them with no opportunity to have input. Ladybird felt like she could not deal with this any longer. This Church was her only family. Her own family had disowned her and she had not spoken to her mother in quite some time. Her father was nowhere around. She had been abused mentally, physically, and sexually. All she wanted was for someone to love her. Ladybird loved receiving praise from her leader. She told me that she felt good when her leader was pleased with her. It came to the place where before Ladybird did anything, she consulted with her leader. She never even thought about asking God. I asked her, "Did you pray over this?" She implied, "Well, I have always assumed that if my leader told me to do this then God must want me to do this." So I proceeded to ask, "Well then, what is the problem." She says, "I feel a tug. This time what I am being told to do does not feel right." After talking for a while, I found out that when Ladybird first arrived at this church, she felt God leading her to a particular area. However, the leadership constantly steered her away from that area. Because she desired to please leadership, she did as she was told. What she had become was not what God wanted for her but what her leader made her become. Little by little Ladybird ceased seeking God and relied totally on her leader. She no longer sought God for herself. She admitted to me that she could not remember the last time she consulted God! All she could ever think about is what her leader thought about what she was doing. It did not matter if God was pleased because she just wanted to please her leader.

At this point, I feel the tugging of the Holy Ghost to clarify something. **I am in no way accusing ALL PASTORS OR PEOPLE IN LEADERSHIP** of being this way. There are those who mean well but were trained and mentored by others who had a congregation full of people pleasers. However, I have no doubt and I will shout to the world that there are **wolves in sheep's' clothing!** Godly Leaders will carry out their duties just as shepherds watching over their sheep. The shepherd knows the needs of all the sheep in their care and guides them accordingly. Godly leaders know the needs and purposes of those entrusted to their care through relationship. Godly leaders guide those under their care towards God's divine purpose. In other words, Godly leaders don't kill purpose, they help bring it about by helping others find and activate God's plan for their lives.

I have come to realize that many people come to church because they have needs. Many of them are hurting and yearning for someone to nurture and love them. Sometimes, they have had either a troubled childhood or no childhood at all. They reach out to anything or anyone that *appears* to love them and do whatever is necessary to keep them in their lives. Unfortunately, many times it means doing and becoming whatever leaders want. This consequently snuffs out the individual's divine purpose and replaces it with a "people induced" purpose. What also ends up happening is the person begins to emulate others. This person will begin to operate within the church like someone else, most likely the Leader, and will even begin to have similar behaviors. Eventually, the predestined purpose for this person is buried. This stronghold not only snuffs out purpose but it places the individual in bondage to the person they are trying to please.

      The stronghold and bondage of people pleasing also exists in the homes. I was enlightened to this from the lives of young people that my husband and I have ministered to over the years – some in church, some not. Many of them hardly ever thought about what they should be doing. To them they are just doing "whatever". To them, there was no such thing as purpose. They just did as they were told, even if it was something they did not want to do. I am not talking here about those who are in Godly obedience to their parents but cases of "just not wanting to upset the parents." As one young man told me, "I just did not feel like dealing with the drama." Yes, we understand that children must obey their parents in the Lord. But, what happens when a parent has no idea of their child's purpose and through their demand for obedience snuffs out characteristics placed by God in that child for their purpose? Let me give an example.

Growing up, I had a lot of mouth; at least that is what I was told. If anything needed to be said you could guarantee that I would say it. If someone needed to hear the truth, I nominated myself to tell him or her. My parents, who understood my purpose, guided me in a way that molded and shaped this boldness within me. They taught me by example, that there was a time and season for everything. This included a time to speak and a time to be quiet. There were times in which Mom popped me in my mouth for being disrespectful or stepping out of line. There were other times in which she informed me that the problem was not WHAT I said but HOW I said it. Both my parents taught me that just because I **could** speak did not mean that I **should** speak. Had my parents not understood purpose, they would have been driven to break me or beat it out of me. I would have lived a life of being told to shut up and most likely would have kept everything to myself to please them. That boldness that I would need later in life to fulfill my purpose as an individual, schoolteacher, and even in ministry, would have been snuffed out of me.

I remember the conversation that I had with a group of young people. A 19-year old young man from that group said "I just did not want to hear the nagging about how I was going to end up, so I told them what they wanted to hear." The other young people around him shook their heads in agreement. When asked what they wanted to do upon graduation most of them would say an occupation or career that sounded good to everyone around them. Others would answer the question by saying "my mother and father said I should be a . . .", and they named that career. A great portion of these young people ended up rebelling by failing to do anything or by simply wasting their parents' money by failing college. Many detested the "school" experience and struggled all through school but simply went because their parents needed something to brag about. In observing these parents, it appeared that many of them were living through their children. They meant well and desired for their children to have a better life than they did. However, the children felt they were being made into miniature versions of their parents. Little by little, the purposes of these young people were snuffed out and replaced with that of their parents. This too, is a form of people pleasing.

These are examples of people, including parents, influencing purpose. These young people don't have time or don't even know how to seek God's purpose for them because they are too bogged down with everyone else, and not God, telling them what they should do. Many parents do what they do out of love and they feel that they have the child's best interest at heart. However, could there be a point where we as parents go overboard? In Chapter 27 of Genesis we find Rebekah instructing her son Jacob how to steal his brother's birthright. Verses 8-9 says, **"Now therefore, my son, obey my voice according to what I** command you. **Go now to the flock and bring me from there two choice kids of the goats and I will make savory food from them for your father, such as he loves**." She told him to **obey** her and do what he was told. Verses 12-13 say, "**Perhaps my father will feel me and I shall seem to be a deceiver to him; and I shall bring a curse on myself and not a blessing.**" His mother said to him, "**Let your curse be on me, my son; only obey my voice**". Jacob was concerned about doing what he was told. If you look back you will find that Rebekah was the one who suggested the plan to her son. Please note how many times she told Jacob to **obey** only her. Jacob did as he was told. He was being obedient. Later on, Rebekah had to fix the problem because the deceptive plan was discovered and Jacob had to flee for his life. Rebekah's demand for her son's obedience almost cost his life. In her mind, she probably thought she was looking out for his best interest!

When discussing people pleasing in the church and home, there is one word that continues to surface - OBEDIENCE. However, after studying the biblical definition for obedience it appears that we, at church and in the home, have been doing something wrong. After reviewing its definition, it is found that obedience means, "to hear" and heed the instructions of one with whom you are in a relationship. This definition confirms what was said earlier about leaders and their members. A godly leader who is in relationship with those in their care know and understand God's purpose and plan for their lives. Knowing this will enable the leader to instruct them on what to do to accomplish God's will for their lives. When a person understands and activates purpose, they will know what to do and where they are placed in the church.

This is true for the home also. Children are told to obey their parents. Parents need to be in relationship with their children. Being in relationship with the children will enable us as parents to know God's plan for their lives. Only then will they be able to give proper instructions and guidance that will put their children on the road to what God has for them. This is what it really means to "train up a child in the way that he should go." The way that he should go is in the way that God purposed for them. Training involves not only parents modeling a life of purpose but it involves instructing the children in ways that will enable the child to step into their purpose. If they are trained in this way, when they become old (matured) they will not depart from this.

The bottom line is that God must be in control of your life. If you are overly concerned with how others feel, then those "others" are in control of your life. They define who you are and if it is not dealt with, they will determine who you will become in the future. In other words, they create purpose for you.

How do we deal with people pleasing? First, you must know who you are and whose you are. If your mind is constantly preoccupied with what people think, you may need to shed these relationships until you understand where God is taking you. If you find yourself seeking the advice of people more than advice from God then you are in need of deliverance from people pleasing. Please listen and hear what I am saying! Many of us spent many years feeling lost and purposeless. For years other things were distracting us and people were molding us into who they thought we should be. I have spent many years allowing people to mold me. Others have called me rebellious, out of order, unstable and unsure. They would assume that I didn't know what I wanted. But, I will never forget the day God's word kept leaping out at me saying; "thou shall have no other gods before me." I kept saying to myself, "I don't worship any other god. What did He mean?" Then I remember doing something I was told to do. I knew that I should not have put my hands to it. But I did not want to upset anyone nor did I want to be considered rebellious. At that moment I realized that I never considered how God felt about what I was doing. I dropped to my knees and repented. When I rose from the floor I no longer cared what people thought. I was delivered and set free! The chains and stronghold of people pleasing had lost its grip over my life!

    Listen, it does not matter who it is! It does not matter whether they hold a title in the church, a family member or just plain old acquaintances. If you find yourself consumed about what another person thinks concerning something God has purposed for you, and it never crosses your mind what God wills, that person (peer or otherwise) controls your destiny. You may be in this same **predicament** and right now you have made up your mind that you would rather please God than man. Well, guess what? Praise God there is freedom and hope for you right now. The Bible says to **"seek ye first the kingdom of God and His righteousness and all these things will be added unto you."** Go before God right now and ask Him to deliver you from people pleasing. Ask Him to direct you towards His purpose for your life. Pray and ask for Him to help you to be able to ignore every distraction, no matter what or who it is. When you get up from praying, begin to praise God and consider it done in the Name of Jesus!

CHAPTER FIVE

PASSION: THE FUEL FOR PURPOSE

After you have identified your purpose and are walking in it, at some point you will find that something else is needed to keep it going. It's like having a new car. That car takes you where you need to go. After a while there will come a time when that car will begin to get low on gas. Without gas, the car will cease to run. No matter how new or nice that car is, without the gas it is no good and cannot serve its purpose. So it is with God's purpose for your life. Something else is needed to keep purpose activated and running. This necessary element is called **passion.** Without passion, purpose is like a car without gas. It won't move.

It is important to clarify what passion means. There is "worldly" passion and then there's spiritual passion. In a worldly sense, passion is defined in many ways such as emotions, appetite, an avid interest, and boundless enthusiasm. If we all were to tell the truth we would remember having an avid interest in doing some crazy and sinful things! Many of the things we did caused us to become emotionally involved. It becomes something that we desire and crave. It could be a man or woman, cigarettes, food, alcohol, etc. Whatever or whomever, it makes us feel as though we cannot do without it. That which we are passionate about occupies a lot of our mind, time and money. Passion misdirected can be dangerous and that danger depends upon the intention of the person. Romans 10:2-3 says, **"For I bear them record that they have a zeal of God, but not according to knowledge (3) For they being ignorant of God's righteousness, going about to establish their own righteousness of God."** Here, Paul is talking about people (Israel) who had a zeal or passion not for the things of God but for the things that they had established as being righteous. They had an interest and boundless enthusiasm for what they thought was righteous living. They were emotionally involved and had a desire for what they believed was righteous living. Many of us have spiritually and physically tossed and turned regarding what we should be doing. We have prayed and sought God and still felt as though we had no answer. Feeling lost, we allowed ourselves to become victims of people speaking into us callings or ministries. After being told what we should be doing we spend a lot of effort, time, emotions and interest into this so-called calling. This enthusiasm is called passion. However, it is very important to know our purpose so that we can become passionate about doing the right thing.

To make things clearer allow me to use gasoline as an analogy for passion. As we all know, we must go to the gas station from time to time to get gas. Gasoline, in this analogy represents passion. The gasoline is made and stored in refineries. The refinery, the place where it all comes from represents God. At the refineries, service trucks fill up before delivering gas to various gas stations. The holding place for the gasoline at a station is a tank. The tank releases the gas through a tube with a handle called a pump.

One day while meditating, this analogy came to me. Gasoline represents passion. The service truck is the Word of God that delivers the gas to the various stations, the place where we reside. We are the cars (instruments/tools) that need passion (gas) in order to do what God predestined for us to do. The tank represents the Holy Ghost, which holds the passion. It will release the passion through the tube, which represents the "line" of prayer. Through prayer we summons the power and anointing of the Holy Ghost. Once we have realized that we have spiritual credit, because Jesus has already paid the price, we can lift the handle. This handle represents our praise and worship and then the passion (gasoline) will begin to flow within us. There is no limit with our credit so we can fill up! Guess what? We can return whenever we need to! Praise God!

Putting passion behind the wrong purpose is like having two cars and putting gas into the one that you are NOT driving. You are not going to make it far in the one car by putting gas in the other. There are many people who do not wait to hear from the Lord, so they end up spending much energy and time doing something that is not going to last. Those of us who have this problem are guilty of telling folks that "God told me to do . . . (whatever it is)." We become passionate about this and before long we are emotionally involved. Before long, that very thing to which we have misdirected our passion begins to die, and the next thing we say is God told us to do something else." Somehow God changes His mind. The problem with passion behind the wrong purpose is that it causes us to waste time. Time that could have been used to further what God predestined for us. Those of us at the age of 40 and over could have found purpose much earlier but had to get off the exit because we took the car without any gas - we filled up the wrong car. With this, two things happen: (1) Hopefully we are close enough to walk back; or (2) we have to wait for help. If we recognize that we are doing the wrong purpose early enough, then the way back is not far. However, there are those of us who have ventured so far out doing the wrong thing that many times, it is going to take someone who knows exactly where we are to come and get us. Like AAA, the automobile association, there are those with whom we are in relationship that have insight into where we need to go. Whenever we experience a "break down" they know just where we are. God places these people in our lives. These people are open to the voice of the Lord and the only interest they have in you is what God has for YOU.

We need spiritual passion in order to carry out God's plan for our lives. This involves a driven motivation and attitude for something that you know is sure. Passion will enable us to have a strong and forceful devotion along with a strong love for whatever it is we are called to do.

As I look back over my life, no matter where I go or live, I am always drawn to the same areas. They are youth, young adults, troubled men and women, rejected people, and the unwanted. We have lived in three different states and we always end up working in those areas. The music ministry sometimes served as a tool that led us to these areas. I have been frustrated, discouraged, and many times ready to quit before my season ended. Every time I was about to quit, that very same day I was somehow back operating in those ministries. There were people who I have said that I was never going to be bothered with anymore. Of course, it did not last. Something within me kept pushing me back into it. In other words, passion produces a desire and a determination within you to do all and be all you can for Christ despite how you feel. When we are induced with passion we can't help but do what God has called us to do. Even when we feel like quitting or giving up, something draws us back.

When we have godly passion we are committed to carrying out our purposes and we will always desire to give God the praise and credit for what HE placed inside us to do. There is someone reading this and the problem you are having is that you need to refuel. You have been trying to drive purpose on an empty spirit. You have no enthusiasm, motivation, or interest in what you KNOW God wants with you. It is time to fill up again. Right now I rebuke everything that has caused you to "park". You shall live and you WILL NOT die. Get up right now and begin to pray. Then begin to praise and worship Him thus releasing your passion. In order for you to stay fueled with passion, you must get in His Word so that the tank never runs out. Do it now! You've got places to go and people to see! There's a world out there full of people who are in need of what God has placed inside you. Your God-given purpose is not only for you to be blessed. It is there to bless others as well. There is no time to waste! Once you have "passioned up", then throw yourself into drive and press on the pedal hard. Go, child go!

CHAPTER SIX

THE KILLERS OF PURPOSE

So far we have covered those elements needed to get us going on this road to purpose. We have even evaluated our own heart, making sure that what we are doing is what **GOD** ordained for us to do.

However, just as with anything else there are spirits in this world whose sole purpose is to hinder the things of God from going forth. John 10:10 says that the thief (Satan) comes to steal, kill and destroy. The mistake that we as believers make is that we assume that the devil will always be obvious in his attack. But the fact that the word says that he comes to steal, kill and destroy indicates that it is possible that he can attack while we are unaware of his tactics. The word steal indicates that he can take from you without your knowledge. To kill means to put an end to your life or whatever makes you live. In the Greek this word means to "undo" (Vines Expository). It also means to nullify and make inoperative. In reference to purpose, this scripture inform us that the enemy, when we least expect it, can take our purpose (the very element that makes you live) and put an end to it by undoing, nullifying and making it inoperative. Little by little, this tears down and destroys a person.

When it comes to our purpose the enemy works hard to place stumbling blocks in our way. When we operate in divine purpose we are using a God ordained weapon, which enables us to tear down the kingdom of darkness. Therefore, he must find a way to snuff out our purpose. So, what does he do? He uses tactics such as temptation, reminding us of past failures and sins, condemnation, etc. I have found that one of his most powerful tactics is CONDEMNATION. He gets a person to focus on their areas of weakness and then, through the tactics listed above, gets them to deem themselves unworthy of forgiveness, deliverance or doing what God has purposed for them to do. This, in turn, hinders the person from focusing on God's purpose and plan for their lives. What happens next? They end up snuffing out themselves! I call this "**spiritual suicide**".

After thinking back on my life and talking with others, I have found some areas that many of us have in common. These areas become the doors that the enemy comes through. Once he gains entrance, he begins to set up residence there until he is either kicked out or until he has accomplished his own purpose.

As we begin to study the following "poisons" of purpose, do a self-evaluation. Look for the areas (or doors) in which the enemy has access and is able to destroy purpose in your life. When those areas are exposed, ask God to help you close every door to which the devil has access and give you the strength and wisdom to keep them closed. Through the Holy Ghost you will be "more than a conqueror" and empowered to stand against anything that comes to destroy what God has placed inside of you.

DISTRACTIONS
SUFFOCATION OF PURPOSE

Once you make a decision to walk in God's purpose for you, things begin to "pop-up" in your life. Is there something that you constantly think about doing and every time you purpose to do it something comes up? These things are called distractions. Distractions are those things or people who are able to draw your attention and focus away from something you should be doing. Spiritual distraction draws your attention away from what God wants you to do or desires you to have.

I am dealing with this problem right now. I have been attempting to write this book for quite some time. But, as soon as I sit down to write, something comes up and before I know it I have forgotten to do what God wanted me to do. Distractions have a way of entering our lives through various avenues. These distractions are NOT always obvious. We must realize that in order for it to be a distraction it has to capture our attention with something that interests or appeals to us.

My time is extremely limited because I work and do a lot of other things. When I get home it is time to do homework with the children. Afterwards it is time to feed the children and then prepare for the next day. There also has to be time to spend with my husband, and let us not forget all the "church activities" during the week. Along with these daily activities, I have to find time for those other areas of purpose in my life. But, every time I sit down to attend to these "divine assignments" something comes up or something "of interest" comes on the television. Before I know it, I am wrapped up in these things and once again, like so many times before, I've missed an opportunity.

There are so many "life" issues that keep our minds preoccupied. However, many of those situations could be controlled. The only reason they can divert our attention is because we allow them to. We give in to these distractions. Truthfully, if we were to look back on those things that destroyed or had the potential to destroy us we would all admit that all we had to do was ignore them. But, its power appeared too great to ignore.

Whether it is watching television, fussing kids, telephone calls, or whatever, if you cannot complete what God wants because something else occupies your time, you are being distracted. Whatever causes you to put down or stops you from finding or walking in purpose is a distraction.

Distraction or diversion does not only come in the form of a physical activity, but it can also be in the mind. There were many days where I had purposed to do something but I could not even focus on the task at hand. In my mind were things, which used up all of my mental spaces. There was no more available space in my mind. This "overcrowding" range from things like worrying about how I was going to do what God was calling me to do, to overanalyzing it into something more complicated than it really was. There were days when I did not get to think about God's plan or what He wanted because my mind was too preoccupied with life problems.

I find myself thinking about all of the things that I felt God wanted me to do but somehow I got distracted. I will never forget what happened to me a few years ago. There was a friend of mine who was in the hospital. She was dying from AIDS. I held a very busy schedule but I felt something moving me to go and see her soon. One day she sent a message by a family member that she needed to talk to me. That day, I was on my way and was immediately distracted by an issue that came up. Well, I thought I would just go the next day. A relative said to me, "I don't believe she knows the Lord as her Savior." This reinforced in me that I had to get there soon. The next day work was extremely stressful. All I could think about was getting home. I became so distracted by all the other things going on that for a while I forgot about my friend in the hospital. I did not remember her until visiting time was over. The next day I had off. I got up early and was preparing to go to the hospital. As I was heading out of the door, the phone rang. My friend had passed away. The pain, grief and guilt that I felt were unimaginable. I knew this was something God wanted me to do, but I had allowed myself to be distracted.

Distraction, which has the potential of constantly stealing our attention, has the power to suffocate God's purpose in our lives. How? That's simple. If our focus is not on what we should be doing, the passion and desire to do it is snuffed out little by little. Before long, you will begin to notice that whatever you were doing you are now doing it less and less. Then one day, you realize that it had been such a long time since you had done anything. Before long, it appears dead. As a matter of fact, it probably is dead.

Many of you may feel that you are not distracted from purpose because all you think about is doing whatever it is God has called you to do. However, for many of you the problem is you are **confused** about what it is you should be doing. Not have I only encountered this personally, but I have ministered to people who constantly go through this type of distraction. You may be saying how is confusion a distraction? If you are not sure of what you should be doing then you are most likely not doing much. What makes something a distraction is that it keeps you from doing whatever it is you should be doing. If you are confused, how could you know what to do? Usually, when a person does not know what to do, then they do nothing.

This was another area that almost kept me from moving forward. I can remember when I first began to operate in what I believed was my God-given purpose. It was not long before I became unsure about whether or not what I was doing was of God. Not only were people "prophesying" something different but also my mind had thoughts that were contrary. At the same time I was dealing with life issues that left me feeling unsure of everything. Here I was doing all that I could to please God but was still struggling financially which in turn caused nothing but drama in my life. I began to question, "What happened to all the blessings that I was supposed to receive as a result of doing God's will?" This left me feeling confused! So what did I do? I stopped doing everything! No wonder I was messed up! Wallowing in confusion kept me distracted from purpose. The scripture says, **"God is not the author of confusion but of peace."** (1 Corinthians 14:33).

While studying, I found out that the source of all types of distractions appears to take place in the mind. Diversions take up physical and mental space thus making it difficult for the person to not have time to do or think about whatever it is they should be doing.

Confusion and any distractions occupy the mind with thoughts that perplexes the person. Confusion has the mind in mental chains, which keeps the person in bondage. Other distractions monopolize a person's time as well as their mind. These types of bondage keep the person from moving on thus suffocating and killing purpose.

Hopefully you have noticed how all of the examples of distraction used, started in the mind. According to Vines Expository, the word mind is defined in the three ways in the New Testament: (1) indicates thought, judgment or a way of thinking, (2) indicates one's perspective or capacity to perceive and (3) represents the faculty used to organize or make sense of perceptions and experiences." Paul captures the danger of a mind that is not of God in Romans 8:6-7. He says, **"For to be carnally minded is death; but to be spiritually minded is life and peace. Because the carnal mind is enmity against God; for it is not subject to the law of God, neither indeed can be."** There are times when the thoughts in our mind become so powerful that we succumb to and then act on those thoughts. We then become so concerned with what is on our minds that it begins to take priority in our lives. There are times when God "gives us over to the reprobate mind" because we are bent on doing what our mind tells us, thus making whatever is in there "lord" over our lives.

As we continue with other examples of *"killers of purpose"* it will be shown how the mind is the holding place for these spiritual diseases. The mind, if we allow, can become the entrance to these killers of purpose that come just like a thief to steal, kill and destroy what God has purposed for us. Let's use a few more examples to expose of these killers of purpose.

PROCRASTINATION
THE "SILENT" KILLER

"**I'll do it tomorrow**." How many times have you said this? Many of us say this statement with the intention of doing whatever it is the next day. However, tomorrow turns into weeks, months, and often years. Putting things off is called procrastination.

Procrastinator was my middle name. I procrastinated with those things that I knew God wanted me to do. As a matter of fact, I procrastinated doing a lot of things. Ironically, I've helped a lot of other people do what it was God wanted *them* to do. But when it came to *my* purpose or me doing God's will for my life, I would constantly put it off. There was always a reason why I could not do it.

As I reflect back over the years of my life I am so ashamed at all of the "unfinished" projects that I have put off. Procrastination becomes a habit or a spirit that becomes the way in which a person's life is governed. When a person procrastinates they don't realize how their purpose is quietly being suffocated. Suffocation involves a cutting off of something that is necessary in order to live. The object being suffocated does not die quickly but slowly, little by little.

It was nothing for me to put off doing things. But one day I came across a passage of Scripture that opened my eyes. In the book of Luke, Jesus defines those who "put off doing" as those who are **"not fit for the kingdom."** In chapter 9 verses 59-62 it says, "**Then he said to another, "Follow me." But he said, "Lord let me first go and bury my father." (60) Jesus said to him, "Let the dead bury their own dead, but you go and preach the kingdom of God." (61) And another also said, "Lord I will follow you but let me first go and bid them farewell who are at my house. (62) But Jesus said to him, "No one having put his hand to the plow, and looking back is fit for the kingdom of God.** To be associated with "being unfit for the kingdom" rocked my world!

Proverbs 27:1 instructs us not to presume in tomorrows because you don't know what tomorrow may bring. Many of us have made so many excuses, which is really a spirit of procrastination within us. Many of you reading this know exactly what God wants you to do. However, every time you attempt it or think it's time to do what God has purposed you talk yourself out of doing it. Many of you have the same problem as I once did. You are so busy helping others fulfill their purpose that you constantly put yours off. Let me clarify something here. We should help our brothers in sisters in carrying out their purposes. However, our assistance should NOT be at the expense of what God has instructed us to do. Yes, there may be seasons in your life where God has you assisting others as a learning process for you. But, if you spend time past those seasons doing the same thing and never move towards what God has for you then there is a problem. Despite what anyone says, God has called us (each one of us) with a holy calling…before time began (2 Timothy 1:9).

When I think about the things in which I procrastinated, I begin to realize how the mind played a major role in assisting me in putting things off. When I put off things, I have to justify or find reasons why I cannot do whatever it is I should be doing. The thought process involves the mind. Don't believe me? Think about the last time you said you were going to do something. When it was almost time for you to do whatever it was, your mind became flooded with many thoughts like **"I'm tired or I'll have more time tomorrow. I have a few days off from work, or it's too early", etc."** Sounds familiar? I can guarantee you that all of the excuses began in your mind. The more you thought about it, the more you convinced yourself that you made the right decision. You might actually have a justified reason for putting it off. However, when procrastination becomes a normal habit, then you are slowly killing your purpose. How? Putting off means you are not doing what God has predestined for you to do. That means you are not doing your purpose. A life without purpose is not a life. You simply exist.

In order for purpose to live you must feed and nourish it. This comes through you studying the Word, fasting and praying, and then activating your gift. Purpose is alive when you are walking in it. Therefore, if you are putting it off, then purpose is not being activated, the passion is not being sparked and your purpose is lying dormant.

Procrastination gives way for other things to settle in your life. Many times there are issues that contribute to the reason why a person procrastinates. They include things like **fear, intimidation and doubt.** Even though they are defined separately, they can work in conjunction with one another. **Fear** is something that weakens and paralyzes a person. It steals a person's determination thus crippling and rendering them helpless and weak. This issue begins in the mind and is heightened by what we think about. When people are fearful about something, they will find some way to talk themselves out of it, or put off what they should be doing. It is amazing to see the number of Christians who are gifted and anointed but they are bound by fear. This fear could be as a result of past failures, rejection, insecurity, low self-esteem or self-worth. Some put off doing something when they compare themselves to others. This fear, which also takes place in the mind, forces them to procrastinate. Many procrastinate until they are able to overcome the fear, but there are so many others who give in to the fear and do nothing. This is a killer of purpose. Fear not only comes from inside factors, but it also can come from a person being **intimidated** by others.

Intimidation "implies reduction to a state where the spirit is broken or all courage is lost" (Merriam Webster Dictionary). According to various references the individual is frightened into submission and has a sense of inferiority in the presence of another person. Even though this can be seen as a type of fear, it also can be a separate category because it involves another person. When referring to people, fear can have many other factors but intimidation, when referring to people, normally involves a person being intimidated by another. I have lost count of the number of people who have procrastinated or chose not to do something they were anointed to do because they "can't do it as well as . . . " another person." I am pretty sure if this is not you, there is someone you know who fits this description. There are so many inactive purposes and gifts sitting in the pews every Sunday or just sitting at home. Then we wonder why the church is struggling? A person, who is intimidated by another, usually procrastinates doing what God has called them to do. Many have procrastinated so long that they will not do anything. Eventually, an inactive purpose becomes a dead purpose. Intimidation takes place in the mind.

How? When individuals compare themselves to another, they seemingly **doubt** what God has given them.

Doubt is a "lack of confidence; an inclination not to believe or accept" (Merriam Webster Dictionary). Based on this definition, doubt can be the initiating factor in both fear and intimidation. Those who lack confidence do so because of how they think and feel about themselves. Once again we are back to the mind. When one doubts what God has given them, they will more than likely procrastinate or not do anything at all. Either way, as we have explained earlier, our purpose is destroyed.

Now, I refer to it as the silent killer because most of us feel that as long as we know our purpose, then we will be okay. Without it being activated, it dies little by little. Procrastination sucks the life out of you and your purpose. It is just like an illness. Let me give you an example.

My husband was diagnosed with Congestive Heart Failure (CHF) several years ago. The doctor told him that this was due to untreated high blood pressure over many years. Had he done something earlier it would not have gotten to this point. This ailment is life threatening. Now, he sees his doctor regularly but he has also taken a very active approach towards dealing with the illness. He has to consistently eat right and exercise. If he had not done this, he would not be here today. Prior to finding out about this illness it was slowly but surely killing my husband. He could not afford to put off those necessary changes. When it comes to our purpose, just like a physical illness, it is not enough for you just to know about it. You must do something about it.

Both distractions and procrastination usually take place early on in our walk to purpose. Both last as long as we allow them to. When speaking to others who were distracted or had procrastinated, some felt that it hindered them from walking in their purpose. After becoming aware of these distractions and what it was doing to them, they were able to go on. Even though some time was lost, they were just excited to have the chance to do God's will for their lives.

In speaking to others, I have found that they have reached a critical point as a result of distraction or procrastination. After years of allowing other things to use up their time and energy, many of them no longer desired to walk in purpose. They had simply given up! Giving up, which also starts in the mind, destroys purpose.

GIVING UP
DESTRUCTION OF PURPOSE

We hear a lot about the richest place in the world being the cemetery. In there are many people with great ideas that they kept to themselves – many purposes that were never found. Many of them were people who had given up and thought they had nothing to give or live for.

This giving up is another killer of purpose that takes place in the mind. When a person quits or gives up on something they have, it usually has been pondered over for quite some time. Many of us in the church have justified why we should no longer do something. When we make statements such as, "**My time is up, or it is time for the young people to take over**", we are giving up. This is true, more so, for those who have done nothing but routine things all of their lives. When you give up, or cease to care about your purpose, you will begin to set up routines or habits in order to make you feel as if you are living or doing something useful. Most of what is done simply involves just doing stuff. For example we go home, go to work and then to church. At home, we do household things, at work we do work duties, and at church we do the "church thing." We add duties to our regular routines such as being involved with our children's school, joining various church auxiliaries or groups just for something to do. At home, we juggle our lives trying to work in family time around our children's extracurricular activities. Many times family time is sacrificed because there are days in which there seems to be not enough time. If there are no children then we most likely will just find ourselves doing whatever to occupy the time. Don't get me wrong. It is important to have these things in our lives because they are instrumental to the growth and spiritual nourishment of our family. However, the problem comes when they are just there to fill a routine. At one time, these routines could have been necessary during a particular season in our lives. As a mother I believe in ministering to and taking care of the needs of my family first. But, there is something wrong if the needs or seasons of my family change, but I am bent on doing the same things the same way. For example, the kids are grown and have moved on but we try to live our unfilled purpose through them. When we are living through our children, we try to force them to do all the things we did not do, or we try to keep our grown kids at home. There are many parents who have given up on fulfilling or doing what was inside them to do. Consequently, they spend a lot of time trying to push their children to accomplish their (the parents') purpose. Let me just speak to you parents and those who may feel that you are either "passed" the age or it's too late. As long as you still have breath in your body, you can do whatever it is that God has ordained for you to do. Don't give up.

    Do you remember Sarah? When God told her that she was going to conceive in her old age she thought He was crazy. She laughed! If most of us women were in Sarah's shoes we would have laughed (or cried) too! Genesis 18:11 says, "**Now Abraham and Sarah were old, well advanced in age; and Sarah had passed the age of childbearing**" **(New King James Version).**

She was well passed the age of childbearing but as you all know, God kept His promise. She might have been too old but the purpose inside of her was still "young enough" for God's promise to be fulfilled (see Genesis 12 and Hebrew 11:11). Praise God!

This reminds me of my mother. My mother knew that she was called to preach when she was in her late thirties or early forties. However, during that time the denomination of which she was a part struggled over the idea of female preachers. This did not stop Mom. She began taking classes in theology. I remember going to those classes with her. She was almost 41 or so. As years progressed, the anointing on her intensified. Except for me, all of my brothers and sisters were able to care for themselves; therefore it freed her to go to school. Even those who were not sure of this female preacher issue acknowledged the anointing that my Mom had on her life. She began preaching all over and did not let inability to get the "piece of paper" (license) interfere with what God had called her to do. At approximately age 63, Mom was finally licensed. Did she stop? No! She became even more empowered and walked into her purpose. Up until the day she became ill, Mom did street ministry to the crack infested neighborhoods, visited the sick, held Bible studies, taught Sunday School, preached and set up programs for Nursing homes, served on the Civilian Police Board, etc. Mom could have given up because of the hindrances she encountered, but I never heard her say "I am too old" or "I might as well give up now." As a matter of fact, purpose was the basis of her prayers when she needed healing. I remember hearing her saying in advance; "I come against any sickness or disease that may arise to keep me from carrying out the will of God for my life". I have no doubt in my mind that if she did not have a life with purpose, death would have taken her by now. Purpose gave her something to live for. Even today, purpose drives her determination to get well. As she has told me, "I have *God* things that I must do." She is holding on to the promises of God. Just as the scriptures say, "When God is for you who can be against you" (Romans 8:31). Mom knows she has a purpose and a passion for what she is doing. Therefore, giving up is not an option.

While we are on the road to purpose, it is important to understand that duties and roles in our lives may change. There is nothing wrong with change. Think about David. What David did as a child was a training ground for things to come later on. The principles learned while tending to the sheep were needed in slaying Goliath and being a King. Have you ever thought about what would have happened to David if he had decided to remain a sheepherder for the rest of his life? What might have happened if David were distracted on the way to purpose? What could have happened if David put off fighting Goliath? Or better yet, what would have happened if he had given up during the fight? The consequences are too great to imagine.

There is someone reading this who has given up on doing what God predestined for you to do. You may have legitimate reasons or excuses for feeling the way that you do. These excuses are slowly but surely suffocating your purpose. You make excuses after excuses and then you sit doing nothing and feeling miserable. Wake up! Stop and shake off that spirit! It is not too late. I have always said regarding doing God's will, **"it ain't over until it's over!"** God predestined your purpose therefore He placed everything you need inside of you to get the job done.

There are those of you who have given up because you've been hurt, rejected, and talked about by others. You have allowed others to drive you to the point where you feel it is better to do nothing. Just remember this. Others don't have a heaven or hell to put you in. So why spend so much time trying to impress them? Don't allow anyone to make you give up on what God has called you to do.

There are those of you who are just simply discouraged. You have been waiting a long time for your "season" to come. You feel like you have done everything right and still it seems as if the plan of God for your life is held up somewhere. You have even seen others blessed and moving upward, which leaves you feeling as if you have missed your opportunity. Last year I was so discouraged because it seemed as if I was going nowhere. I was so tired of doing what I believed I was called to do, and yet I was still struggling. I was ready to quit until I turned to the scriptures and realized that I was not the only one who went through this. Job waited a long time before the promises of God for him came to pass. Noah and Abraham's purpose took a long time to come to pass. One thing was certain about all of them; they remained faithful and loyal to the promise of God. Even when they felt like giving up, they didn't. When Job lost his children, home, possessions, cattle, everything, he could have given up. But he said, **"Naked I came from my mother's womb and naked shall I return there. The Lord gave and the Lord has taken away. Blessed be the name of the Lord"** (Job 1:21). Despite his trials and tribulations he declared that **"Though He (God) slay (him) yet will (he) trust Him.** (Job 13:15). I had to understand that purpose is divine, meaning it happens in God's time. God's time is not man's time. God's time means that certain things must be in order in a person's life before the plan of God for them can be released.

As shown earlier, before a person gives up they would think about it for a while. They do not just decide to do so that day or that minute. The mind will begin to ponder over all of the things or issues that bring frustration to the individual. These frustrations build up over a period of time, which eventually immobilizes the individual. The person then feels incapable of doing anything!

What do you do next? Well as it is said, when there is a problem, you go to the source. From distractions to procrastination to giving up, the problem is in the mind.

Remember the Bible speaks of the mind as: (1) one's thought, judgment, or way of thinking and (2) indicates one's perspective or capacity to perceive. Therefore, according to these definitions, the problem is how we perceive what we do. Perception involves how we understand or see what we do. **Proverbs 23:7 say, " For as man thinks in his heart, so is he."** When the Bible speaks of the heart, it is referring to the inner essence of a man, in other words who a person really is. Therefore if you think you are defeated, you become a defeated person and will live a defeated life. If you think that you are poor, you will become poor and you will live in poverty. We need to watch what we allow to get into us. When the spirit of giving up comes upon us we must speak to whatever it is we are quitting, and speak life to it! Renew your mind! **I can do all things through Christ that strengthens me!** (Phillipians 4:13)

Many times, distraction, procrastination, and giving up happen because we lack understanding and insight into what we are or should be doing. The mistake that we make is we only view our purposes simply as "stuff" we do. We don't see or understand how it fits into God's overall plan and how it opens doors for other purposes to be released. Listen, your purpose is the perfect will of God. You will not understand or desire God's will for your life if you don't watch what is in your mind. You need to change your perception of purpose. Romans 12:2 say, "**And be not conformed to this world but be ye transformed by the renewing of your mind, that ye may prove what is that good, and acceptable and perfect will of God**". Lack of insight makes us easily distracted and constant procrastinators, and then we find ourselves throwing in the towel all together.

There are many people who now just exist. They go to church and are very active doing what they have done for years. There are those who have been called to the ministry but are content sitting day after day, week after week, and year after year just doing "stuff". I refer to this as "stuff" because it involves just doing things that have little or nothing to do with their purpose. God has equipped some with great business minds, but they are content working for someone else and not venturing out into what God placed in them. They have given up because of the fear of failure or they are unsure of how their needs will be met. Where is our faith in God?

As for me, had I understood purpose earlier, I would have lived and ministered differently. Had I known what I know now, I could have helped those around me begin to walk in their purpose.

If you are a leader of a ministry, it is important for YOU to understand purpose. This will help those entrusted to your care understand purpose and will help them know what they should be doing. The chance of this happening is extremely low if you as a leader are not walking in your purpose. There is so much more to life than just being "saved" as we in the church have defined it over the years. There is purpose. When a person understands purpose, they do not have to be begged to do their part of God's overall plan. When God's people understand purpose they will become excited because they will have a strong sense of where they are headed, what they have to do, and who they are. With this new lease on life they will realize that they have no time to be distracted, no time to procrastinate and no desire to give up.

THE BACK DOOR

The search for purpose affects people of all ages. Many of you reading this book are (probably) adults or very mature youth. Whether you are young or old there are other ways in which distractions, procrastination and even giving up enters our lives. One such way is through unhealthy relationships.

As was said before, most of us did not find our purposes, if found at all, until later in life. Life situations and circumstances kept many of us distracted thus making our purposes a low priority. Those of us who are married must not only consider the purpose of ourselves, but also that of our spouses and children. For some married couples, finding and activating purpose **may** be difficult to do. But, those of you who are single can, if you chose to, activate your purpose easier and faster than those of us who are married or with children. Many of you have been to single workshops or conferences searching for how to feel complete as a single person. You were reminded that being single was a blessing. You are told how you can do the things of God whenever you want because you have no one but yourself to care for. This may be true. However, being single does not necessarily mean that you are immune to the killers of purpose. There are many of you singles who have placed distractions in your life that have consumed you mentally. How? You fall into one of the following categories: 1) You are consumed with **looking** for a companion; or 2) You are **in a relationship** before discovering purpose. Need further explanation?

    Allow me to introduce Chayrelle. Chay, as she is called, is a 29-year old hairdresser who is very active in church. She is very obedient to her Pastors and loyal to her local congregation. Everyone talks about how Chay has it going on. However, after the shouting, and the benediction is pronounced, Chay goes home to an empty house. That void and empty place in her life drives her to do what she does every night – pray for God to send her a man. Chay is so lonely that this yearning plagues her mind and is a great portion of what she thinks about all the time. Somewhere, Chay feels that she can't go on without a man in her life. What's the problem? Well, all the time that Chay uses up thinking about how much she needs a man is time wasted. Just for the record, this same scenario could apply if this was a 29 year- old man named Chuck who desires a woman!

    I have known many people, over the years, who wanted a mate badly. However, these people did not realize that they were not ready. I had asked many of them what kind of mate they desired. They would describe this "fantasy" person that was made up of great looks, lots of money and the ability to do so much for them. This fantasy person sounded like someone from a television show or movie! In truth, they did not know what kind of companion they wanted or needed. In order for someone to know who they want or need, they must know who they are and where they are going. I remember asking these same people about where they were headed in life – their purpose. The answer - they did not know. People in this kind of predicament do not realize how fortunate they are. Remember, purpose is what gives direction to our lives. With purpose we have a sense of where we are going. What would happen if God gave you this companion and you had not found God's purpose for your life? First of all, you must acknowledge that you are attracting this individual based on where you are at that time. Let me show you what happened with Chay.

One day according to Chay, God answered her prayers. There was a young man who had been visiting her church often. She had noticed him one Sunday as he walked around for the offering. Then one Sunday he joined the church and Chay "claimed him in Jesus' name." She just knew in her spirit that he was the one! Chay was not certain about what God had purposed for her life. There were times when she felt the call to evangelism. But, she loved to do hair. She would become so confused that she would quickly push the thought immediately out of her mind. She, eventually, stopped thinking about it altogether because according to her "He would reveal it to her in due time." At that present time, she was just happy being saved, sanctified and filled with the Holy Ghost.

Chay and her new beau began to date and she worked hard to impress this young man. One night at a revival held at her church, she was called to the front of the church and the guest minister "prophesied" to her that God had called her to be an evangelist. He also told her "the salon would be the place where she would witness and empower people to do the things of Christ." God had finally revealed her purpose. Now that she knew her purpose, she put off doing it feeling as though she had time.

As time went on they became engaged and married shortly thereafter. The honeymoon season soon settled into the realities of married life. Chay had her man but something was still missing.

She thought she would feel complete with her husband. Why was she still feeling incomplete? That is when she realized that she was without a purpose. Her life still had no real meaning. She began to earnestly seek God. She began to spend hours in the Word and in prayer. Being active in church gave her an opportunity to nurture the gift of evangelism in her life. She began to minister to her clients as she did their hair. At the same time her clientele began to grow. It was time for her to open her own shop. People began hearing about Chay by word of mouth. Many spoke of how anointed she was. Eventually, Chay began to get calls to minister. Her husband was not a happy camper! He began to kick up a fuss because his wife, who use to be at home all the time, was now doing more evangelizing, preaching conferences and spending more time at the shop ministering to her clients. In order to keep the peace; Chay began to decline engagements. The stress was too great, so she decided to stop everything, except doing hair. Notice how Chay, through this relationship, experienced all of the "killers of purpose" previously spoken about. Her first experience was allowing herself to be **distracted** by the search for Mr. Man. The next one came when she found God's purpose for her life, but she chose to **procrastinate.** Now being married she came across the most lethal of them all—she was ready to **give up.** The struggle between her husband and church became overwhelming. Her husband began to say he did not marry someone who was in the ministry. He married a faithful, churchgoing young lady. Now he felt as though he was competing for her attention. Needless to say, the fact that he did not know his purpose made the situation even worse. Before long, they both came to a point where they thought there were only two choices: 1) End the marriage; or 2) Give up what she felt was her calling. No matter the choice, each would have a devastating impact.

Many of us were blessed to marry someone who understood purpose. I did not understand purpose until after I married my husband. I was very blessed that his calling was in an area that was compatible to mine and he understood what God had predestined for me to do. Before we started dating, we both had been doing things, which unknown to us happened to be a part of our purpose. This made it easier for us to walk into our purpose during marriage. We both also had a sense of each other's direction. Therefore, as our divine purpose became clearer to us, it was no surprise to either of us.

However, it was still difficult to move forward because I had to learn how to balance time between ministry, children and husband. As our personal relationship with the Lord grew, we entered new levels and seasons of purpose, which required changes in our routines. Based on our perception, it appeared as though one area limited the other. However, the roles and duties of a spouse and parent do not go away because of purpose. As a matter of fact, they are all a part of God's plan for our lives. I do not regret my decision to marry, but I do know that if I had understood purpose before marriage, I would have activated it first, married, then started a family. Let me clarify. It would be to the wonderful man I am married to now (brownie points!) and I would still have all my beautiful children!

If you don't get anything else, please understand that activating your God-given purpose would be **EASIER** if you find your purpose before finding a spouse. However, if it does not happen for you that way, purpose is still attainable. My husband and I, along with many others, are living witnesses of that.

Let us not forget those who are not married but are in a relationship with someone. Your situation is similar to that of Chay's. However, the good thing is you have not married **YET**. If you have not found your purpose it would be wise to slow the relationship down until you do. Your "friend" needs to know where you are going with your life and what will be required of them. The same thing goes for you. You need to know where your "friend" is going and what will be required of you.

It is important to allow God to expose every element of your life while you are single. Marrying before finding out who you are and where you are going in life could very easily set you up in an unhealthy and unsatisfactory relationship which could delay or destroy God's purpose for your life.

There is good news! Whatever state you are in, walking in purpose is always achievable. It may look impossible to you, but Matthew 19:26 informs us that **"with man there may be things that are impossible but with God all things are possible"**. No matter what the enemy places in your way to try to kill your purpose, he cannot kill what God set into motion long before you were born, **unless YOU let him.**

If after reading this chapter you have realized that the enemy has been working hard to snuff out what God placed within you, don't get discouraged. Just praise God because you found him out! Don't worry about the time lost because what the devil meant for bad God can turn it around for your good. Once you've recognized the tools of destruction used by the enemy, purpose will enable you to snatch them and beat him with them! From this day forth you must declare that anything that has the potential to tempt or distract you will no longer be able to do so. You are now focused because you are going to **"set your mind on things above** (those things of God) **and not on things on the earth"** (Colossians 3:2). From this day forth there will be no more procrastination. James 4:14-15 informs us that we do not know what will happen tomorrow. It goes on to say, **"For what is your life? It is even a vapor that appears for a little time and vanishes away. Instead you ought to say if the Lord wills we shall live and do this or that"** (New King James Version). As the saying goes, "we should not put off for tomorrow what we can do today for tomorrow is not promised to anyone. I speak to your spirit right now and declare in the Name of Jesus that you will NOT be distracted, nor procrastinate nor give up. I speak life to your dead purpose and command it in the Name of Jesus to arise! Right now! If you are single, pray that God will help you to walk in your purpose. This is necessary so that when your mate comes into your life, they will know in **advance** who you are and what will be required of them. If you are single and in relationship with someone, pray that God will help you both to walk in divine purpose. If that person does not understand purpose and they are not interested in knowing about it, this is what I would do . . . CHECK IT! This would be a very unhealthy relationship. If you are married, you must pray that you and your spouse find and activate God's purpose for your lives. Pray against everything that tries to come into your marriage to destroy or cause division. In Phillipians 3:12-14 Paul tells how he made it through when it seemed as though he was not going to make it. He was ready to give up. He says, "**Not that I have already attained or am already perfected, but I PRESS ON, that I may lay hold of that for which Christ Jesus has also laid hold of me. Brethren, I do not count myself to have apprehended but one thing I do, FORGETTING those things which are behind and reaching forward to those things which are ahead, I PRESS TOWARDS**

the goal for the prize of the upward (high) call of God in Christ Jesus" (New King James Version). From this day forth you need to make the decision that you are going to press towards the things of God and get all that He has for you. Say and believe, **"NO MORE DISTRACTIONS, NO MORE PROCRASTINATION AND NO GIVING UP IN JESUS NAME.**

CHAPTER SEVEN

PURPOSE AND YOUR LINEAGE

(You Are Not The Only One)

The more I began to understand purpose, the more my perception of life began to change. I kept thinking that what God had purposed for me to do was all about me. As I searched the scriptures, looking for a revelation on predestination, I began to realize an important reality: purpose did not begin with me and it will not end with me. What do I mean?

When studying the scriptures it appears that purpose is carried throughout generations. In order for God's overall plan to be carried out, it appears that where one generation stops another picks up. In Genesis 9: 18-19 it says, **"Now the sons of Noah who went out of the ark were Shem, Ham, Japheth. And Ham was the father of Canaan. These there were the sons of Noah, and from these the whole earth was populated."** Noah's purpose continued down to his children, and from his children to his grandchildren. If you read chapter 10 you will find how the descendants of the three sons would be, eventually, divided up into nations. These nations were to populate the entire earth. But it didn't stop there because it went to his great grandson Abraham. In Chapter 12 of Genesis God informs Abraham that **He would**

"make him a great nation and his name would be made great. In Abraham all the families of the earth shall be blessed." It did not stop there. In Genesis 17:7 God told Abraham that the covenant He made with him will be carried out through his descendants.

Since a person's purpose is based on God's overall plan, it only makes sense that it passes from generation to generation. Why? Purpose comes from the mind of God; therefore it is eternal and not subject to time. However, we have to work within the time given to us.

Each of these "generational purposes" required characteristics or traits given by God and passed down from generation to generation. This is why we need to be careful about how we live and what we say around our children. Let us look at the lives of Noah and Abraham.

Using Noah and Abraham as examples, gives us the ability to look at a small part of God's overall plan unfolding. There were many years between Noah and Abraham. However, when you compare what was required of both, you can see that certain attributes and characteristics necessary for one was also necessary for another. Both Noah and Abraham had to be obedient to God, loyal and faithful, as well as men of faith. When you see the same characteristics in great-grandparents, grandparents, parents and children, those characteristics must have been passed down through each generation, one after another.

God required both Noah and Abraham to leave what was familiar. This meant that they both had to obey and totally trust God. Noah and Abraham were just given instructions, and neither one questioned God. In Genesis Chapter 6: 4, God informs Noah that He wanted him to build an ark. At verses 14-21 God gives specific building and occupancy instructions. Verse 21 says, **"Noah did according to ALL that God commanded him, so he did"**. In Genesis Chapter 12 the Lord went to Abram and told him to leave his home and go to a place that He would show him. At verses 2 and 3 He informs Abram of His purpose for his life. Verse 4 says, **"So Abram departed, as the lord had spoken unto him"**. In other words, Abraham trusted God so much that he just did without question exactly what God had instructed him to do. What God wanted or purposed for them exceeded their imagination. Remember what God told both Noah and Abram? God told Noah that he would be used to populate the earth, and He told Abram he would be Father over a great nation. A promise of this magnitude exceeds one's imagination. Now you must remember that only Noah and his family went in that ark. How was he going to populate the earth with just his family? How was Abraham going to be father over a nation with a wife who was barren? The ability to be that trusting and obedient to God did not just show up in Noah. These traits had to be demonstrated in the lives of the people around these men. Noah was an obedient man and this spirit of obedience was passed down to Abram and so forth.

This made me think hard. Is it possible that God's plan for my life could be carried on through my descendants? When struck with this question I had to begin not just to look at my own purpose but consider the purposes of my children. If I fail to do what God has purposed for me to do, how would this affect the purposes of my children? Pondering over this question made me wonder about the purpose of my parents and grandparents. More questions began to arise in my mind. What were the purposes of my parents and grandparents and so forth? Did they walk in their purposes? Whether they did or did not, how does this affect where I am today? These are legitimate questions. If we were to take a look in the Bible we would notice how one generation's purpose fed right into the purposes of their future descendants. I began to examine what I was doing and how it related to my parents.

I am a schoolteacher. My father and paternal aunts and cousins were all schoolteachers. My maternal grandmother was also schoolteacher. Teaching is what I do as a career but it is also one of the things that I do in the ministry. From both sides, I gained the love and respect for teaching. However, I feel that the love, passion and respect I have for teaching come directly from my father. I remember how thorough and effective he was as a Sunday School teacher. He enjoyed teaching. All those teachers in my family took pride in their teaching positions and this attitude was passed down to me.

As an evangelist I have a lot of the same characteristics as my mother. The passion that I have for the souls of people seems linked to the passion that my mother has as an evangelist. From early on I learned that I must obey God at all times, even if it means defying man-made systems exalting themselves above God. Even though it did not manifest until much later, these standards were instilled in me at a very early age. This willingness to stand on the principles of the Word was a part of both parents' characteristics. They trained all of their children as living examples. We watched and learned from them. I remember during one of my rebellious days informing my parents that when I had children of my own I would never demand from them what my parents demanded from me. My siblings and I would sit around and "crack" on our parents and their old fashion ways! Despite my claim not to be like them I still inherited certain traits that are evident in my life today. I later realized how necessary some of these traits, attitudes, and perceptions are for my purpose. These same traits, attitudes and characteristics can been seen in my children today. I see traits and characteristics of myself, my husband and of our parents in our children. Coincidentally, my in-laws are teachers also. My father-in-law is a very educated man and teaches Sunday school. My mother-in-law is also a retired teacher having taught elementary and secondary all of her career. My children may or may not be teachers or preachers but whatever their purpose, I am sure that the traits, attitudes and characteristics of a teacher will be necessary.

What does all this mean? When you allow something or someone to snuff out your purpose, or if you just decide to blow off this "purpose stuff", you are not only killing your purpose but also the purpose of your children and their children. If your children don't find and activate their purposes, you better believe their children's purposes will also be snuffed. This made me look back at a scripture that I have heard so many times. In Exodus 20:5 God spoke these words, "**you shall not bow down to them nor serve them (idols) For I the Lord your God am a jealous God,** *visiting the iniquity of the fathers upon the children to the third and fourth generations of those who hate me*"**(New King James Version).** Those who worshipped idols passed the teachings and practices of idolatry to their children and grandchildren. Therefore the consequences of the fathers' generation were carried to their children, grandchildren, great-grand children, etc. This cycle will not break until someone decides to do something different – do what God has predestined.

You can usually tell what kind of environment a child comes from by the way he acts. Regardless of how or what you feel about your parents or the ones by whom you were raised, you most likely will have one or more of their characteristics or traits. In First Kings chapter 15, you find the introduction of Abijam, one of David's sons. Abijam became one of the kings of Judah. In verse 3 it says, **"And he (Abijam) walked in all the sins (iniquities) of his father, which he had done before him, and his heart was not perfect with the Lord his God, as the heart of David his father."** As you read on there was not much more said about Abijam's life. Abijam picked up some of his father's ways, however he did receive favor because of his father's (David) relationship with God (see verse 4). God had purposed for Abijam to be a king, just as his father. However Abijam did not gain the heart of God like David, which might have attributed to his unsuccessful reign as king.

After reading this passage of scripture I became more intrigued by how the actions and personalities of prior generations affect not only my generation but also future generations. When people say to me "you look just like your mother or father", I understand more now that they are speaking not just of physical appearances but also mannerisms. The fact that I teach like my father and preach like my mother did not happen because I was trying to be like them. It was characteristics placed in me by God in order to carry out His purpose. Unknown to me, He used my environment to accomplish this. In many ways, the way that I react and respond to my children is similar to that of my relationship with my parents. Although they may say otherwise, it is the same for my siblings. Whenever we get together as a family, it is funny to see how each of us, in our own way, look and act like our parents. Are there any differences? Yes, there are some, which I believe gives our purpose individuality.

I thought further about destructive behaviors that are taught to our children just like those parents of Biblical times who taught idolatry. I began to think of the teachings of hate that we of all races pass down from generation to generation. Prejudice is not something that people are born with, but it is injected into their hearts through environment. Prejudiced parents produce prejudiced children. If the children are unable to break from this, the cycle and the consequences will continue. Prejudice is just ONE example of many but there are so many more behaviors, traits and characteristics where this principle applies.

After studying what we have just read in Exodus and First Kings, I began to search myself. Before reading this, I had it in my mind that whatever I did was not going to hurt anyone but myself. This passage showed me that I could no longer proceed down this purposeless road and set up a life of mere existence for my children. Jesus came so that we might have life and have it more abundantly. In other words, He came so that I would be able to do all that He purposed for me. This includes my physical, mental, emotional, financial, and spiritually development. Without purpose I am passing down a life of spiritual poverty to my children. This poverty would involve a lack of spiritual insight, perseverance and spiritual hunger for the things of God. Most of all, it would mean a life void of their part in God's overall plan.

Just like Noah and Abraham it is the duty of my husband and me to find and do our purpose, which serves as a model (training) for our children. Listen, when the bible instructed us parents to **"train up a child in the way that he should go",** this deals with the child's purpose. God gave my husband this revelation. Training up a child in the way that a child should go means that as parents, we should place them on the road to their purpose, God's predestined plan for *their* lives. Remember purpose is what gives direction and meaning to our lives. The scripture goes on to say **"when they are old they will not depart."** The word "old" does not only mean chronologically old but it also means "maturity". So, this scripture can be interpreted as this. ***Illustrate for and direct your children in the ways that will show them God's plan for their lives, and when they are mature, they will walk in it on their own.*** After experiencing God's perfect will for your life, who would want to leave it?

It is time for all of us to take seriously how our actions affect the lives of our descendants. What you are doing or not doing right now will bring consequences (good or bad) to our children and grandchildren. We can no longer take a selfish attitude or position toward the decisions and actions of our lives. We can no longer sit back and assume that we are only hurting ourselves. We are hurting others also. Just think of the effect on each generation. If I do not walk into my purpose, will my great-great-great-grandchildren face an even greater possibility of being purposeless? This is a question to be considered. I know that I do not want to take that chance and risk destroying the lives of my future generations. All that matters is that God created me with a specific purpose in mind and because it is my desire to please Him I must be willing to walk in it. This Spirit of obedience is what I desire for all of my children and their children. If I teach them to love God then they will keep His commandments. If they know to keep His commandments, then they will do as He says. If they do as He says then they will know His purpose for them.

It is important for you to stop right now and examine your life. If you have allowed someone or something to kill God's purpose for your life, God wants to revive it again, if you let Him. He is a God of chances even if it is your first, second, third or fourth! It's not over until it's over! Do you think it is too late? NO! He can do exceedingly and abundantly above all you can ask or think! Make a decision right now and take back your life, the life of your children, and your grandchildren! Restore purpose to your lineage.

CHAPTER EIGHT

<u>THE POWER OF PURPOSE</u>

As we come to the conclusion of this book, it is so important for you to understand that purpose is such a powerful tool. Purpose, as said many times through this book, is what gives direction, meaning and substance to one's life. Without purpose, we are like the Israelites wandering around in the wilderness, knowing about the Promised Land, but never doing what it takes to get there. Not because we don't know how, but for the most part, we don't want to do what it takes to get there. God has given us distinct instructions through the Word of God on how to access our purpose. It is gained through our relationship with God. When we are in relationship with God, then we are aware of what He desires for us to do. It is just that simple. There are no twelve steps. Once we have established our relationship with God, all we have to do is be obedient to His instructions. When we are obedient to His instructions, all that He desires for us will be ours. But let me warn you. When you are walking where God wants you to, expect those around you who are not walking in their own purpose to become your "nay-sayers". I was feeling this way and was unsure about why? However, I received my confirmation through the Word of God.

In Genesis 26:12-34, you find a man by the name of Isaac. Isaac was obedient to the instructions of God. Isaac sowed in the land called Gerar where Abimelech was king and he also reaped that same year. The Lord blessed him, as He promised, and he prospered greatly. The Philistines, because of envy, stopped up the wells Isaac had built. Eventually, Abimelech told Isaac to leave because he had more than everyone else did.

You know when you are on the road to purpose when your greatest obstacles seem to come from those who have been around you. I did encounter this problem. It seemed like EVERYTIME I was being blessed, there were those "haters" (as the young people say) who envied what God was doing in my life, fearful that I was going to have more than they have. If you read the whole chapter of Genesis 26 you will find this was one of the problems with Abimelech and the Phillistines towards Isaac. I experienced these feelings from friends, family, church members and other associates. Say Amen somebody!

However, I must say that this is not always a bad thing, as you will see with Isaac. These people made him leave, but God turned it around for his good. In verse 17 Isaac left from his home, with his wives and children and went to the valley of Gerar where God continued to bless him. Reading further through verse 20 you will find that he continued to find opposition there. There were "haters" who felt that he was getting more than they were. I can relate to this because I no longer live in the home of my birth. In 1998 my husband and I knew that it was time to leave that land. As we look back over the years we realized much of the opposition we encountered was the same wherever we went. However, God was using those situations to remove those things in our lives that would hinder us from reaching and activating His will for our lives. In order for us to liberate God's people, we had to be freed ourselves. During these times of purging, He had shown how many others, including us, were more concerned with people than God. God began to use us mightily, especially in the area of exposing those areas within a church where people are in bondage to man-made laws that were rituals and not biblically based. Their convictions were not based on a relationship with God and had not penetrated their hearts. Their convictions were originated and controlled by other men. Many times I was so ready to quit until the scriptures reminded me that I was doing the will of God and not man. Therefore, I should not seek the applause of man but the applause of God.

Continuing in Genesis 26 you will find a place of victory in this story. Isaac continued to dig wells but kept encountering opposition. Eventually, he moved and dug a well that his opposition did not quarrel over. He called this well Rehoboth, which meant "spacious" because God had made room for them to dwell there. He went from there to Beersheba and God, once again, confirmed His promise to him. Abimelech, the king who told Isaac to leave in the first place, went looking for Isaac. He found him in this place called Beersheba. Isaac asked him, **"Wherefore come ye to me, seeing ye hate me, and have sent me away from you? (28) And they said, We saw certainly that the Lord was with thee; and we said, Let there be now an oath betwixt us, even betwixt us and thee, and let us make a covenant with thee."** The king who earlier told Isaac to leave now wanted to be in covenant with him. When you walk in purpose you are not the only one blessed but all that are around you are blessed. Even your enemies, just like with Isaac, will desire to walk with you because they would see the blessings of the Lord upon you. Isaac continued, from that day on, to be blessed. Now don't forget, Isaac's children had to go through this with him. They went through the trials of moving with their father. However, because of his obedience they reaped the blessings too. Even though my husband and I continued to get opposition, we continued to listen and obey the voice of God There were times when we felt discouraged because it seemed as if we had been struggling for so long. We had to look to the Word of God to cut that feeling of discouragement out of our lives. We turned to the scripture that said, **"Let us not be weary in well doing for in due season we shall reap, if we faint not" (Galations 6:9).**

There are some of you who have moved and no matter where you are; you are faced with many obstacles. You must hold on to what you know that God has spoken in your life. What do you think would have happened to Isaac had he given in to all the complaints and jealousies of those people? He would have missed what God had for him. I realized that I have been on this road too long to turn back or give up now. I am too close to my blessings. You must speak the word of God in your life and like Paul begin to edify yourself. If life or death is in the power of the tongue, then use that instrument to speak life unto yourself. You are too close to get off the road now. Just think, the day you give up may be the day God delivers your blessing. There were many days that I sat and felt discouraged about how long I had been on this road. I use to ask God all the time, when am I going to reap the harvest of my labor? How is it that my purpose involved helping people move to their next level, yet I am still struggling in so many ways? Some days I felt this war going on in my spirit. One day while praying God spoke these words: **"All I need is one second to change your life. What takes man a lifetime to accomplish I can do in the blink of an eye, because I am God! What takes man many generations to accomplish I can do faster than the speed of light. Why? I am God. What you may consider impossible is possible with me. Why? Because I am God."** Now, I give these words to you. Don't give up. Your life and the life of your family depend on what you do and how you do it. You are about to get to the place of Rehoboth, the place where God has made room for you. You are about to set up your tent in your Beersheba; and all those who have a problem with what God is doing will want to be around you because they realize that all who are in your company are also blessed.

As of right now you possess all that it takes to get your purpose moving. You should have built a relationship, obeyed the voice of the Lord and rid your life of all those things that would kill your purpose. Parents, at this point you should be building relationships with your children and seek God for the purposes of your children. You now have understanding and are aware of all of the snares that were set by the enemy to kill your purpose. You know that if your purpose is killed, you and your descendants will be purposeless and simply exist. You have fueled your purpose with passion and are ready to go and take back what the devil has stolen from you. At the same time you will be salvaging all the purposes of your descendants. Right now you should be liberated and emancipated because those chains of distraction, procrastination, giving up, people pleasing, fear, intimidation, and doubt are broken. All PURPOSE-KILLERS are being executed! You should be free, for the Word says, **"Whom the SON sets free is free indeed"** (John 8:36). No other person or system can set you free. You are free when you follow the principles of the Bible, the liberating Word. From this day, you are released in the Name of Jesus. The pages of God's Word are your emancipation papers. When Jesus died on the cross and conquered death, He broke the chains. Go forward never again to return to the place of bondage. Today, you are free! Praise God! You Are Free Indeed!

AETOS MINISTRIES INTERNATIONAL comprises the various ministries of Anthony & Rhonda Ferguson.

These ministries include Book Writing & Publishing, Songwriting, Music Recordings & Live Presentations, Speaking Engagements, Dance & Music Instruction, Counseling, Youth Ministry and Finance.

For more information or bookings, e-mail us at:

aetosmi@aol.com